FINDING MYSELF

FINDING MYSELF

BEYOND THE FALSE BOUNDARIES
OF PERSONAL IDENTITY

Arnold Zuboff

Special supplement to
Midwest Studies in Philosophy

Philosophy Documentation Center
Charlottesville

Finding Myself: Beyond the False Boundaries of Personal Identity

by Arnold Zuboff

© 2025 Arnold Zuboff and *Midwest Studies in Philosophy*

ISBN 978-1-63435-117-1

Library of Congress Control Number: 2025948266

Published 2025 by the Philosophy Documentation Center.

Philosophy Documentation Center
P.O. Box 7147
Charlottesville, Virginia 22906-7147
www.pdcnet.org

This volume is the first of a series of original monographs to be published by the Philosophy Documentation Center as special supplements to *Midwest Studies in Philosophy*, ISSN 1475-4975. Each supplement is to be published open access online, with a CC BY-NC-ND license. Income from the journal will support open access publication of each supplement without cost to the author.

Print copies will be available on demand at modest cost.

FOREWORD

I got to know Arnold Zuboff when he was a graduate student at Princeton and I an assistant professor, and I have followed the course of his thoughts with fascination ever since. He has always impressed me as a philosopher of exceptional depth, originality, and skill. Those qualities are manifest in the work before you. Zuboff has been developing and refining his ideas about the self for many years, and it is very gratifying to see them finally embodied in a book.

Zuboff proposes and defends with creative philosophical arguments a radically original conception of the mind, according to which the distinction between selves—between me and you, for example—is an illusion. There is only one subject of consciousness; it is the subject of all consciousness, and it is equivalent to the first-person immediacy shared by all conscious experience. The separate bundles of experience in the lives of distinct conscious organisms do not have separate subjects, but share a universal quality of subjective immediacy, which it is easy for each of us to mistake for a unique individual "I" in our own case. To mark the universality of the "I" Zuboff calls his theory *universalism*. He makes this transformative idea vivid and intelligible, and argues for its truth on probabilistic grounds that are original and of great philosophical interest. Amazement at one's own existence, given its apparently stupendous objective improbability, proves to be the starting point for a profound exploration of many philosophical problems.

Both the conclusion and the argument will certainly seem incredible, even outrageous, to many readers, but the whole is presented with such care and skill that it should be regarded as an important contribution even by those who are not persuaded. The relation of the mind to the world is so mysterious that it is not philosophically reasonable to dismiss any view, however radical, out of hand. The conclusion that the distinction between selves is an illusion seems to me, in advance, as eligible a view as any, and the probabilistic argument for the conclusion is fascinating and ingenious.

This is a very unorthodox book, and Zuboff does not write in an orthodox academic style, but in my view it is a philosophical contribution of the first order. Zuboff writes with beautiful clarity, and the overall argument, though conceptually difficult, comes across in an accessible way. Zuboff is a true original; his ideas merit the closest attention.

Thomas Nagel
University Professor Emeritus
New York University

For you—the one with all the bodies and minds

FINDING MYSELF

BEYOND THE FALSE BOUNDARIES
OF PERSONAL IDENTITY

CONTENTS

*In what follows I will be talking a lot about what I am. 'It is I' is formally correct;
but 'It is me' sounds more natural—and I will often be using the latter.*

A little advice about reading this book: I am, of course, trying to make
everything clear. But if you ever feel bogged down, please move on (and
maybe come back to that later). I am confident you will still get lots of
what I am saying.

A Brief Proof That You Are Every Conscious Thing

Know thyself—Oracle of Delphi

Imagine that you wake up and learn that this awakening was the result of one of two alternative 'awakening games' having been played.

In the 'hard game' you would have been awakened only if a fair coin that was flipped a thousand times happened to have matched precisely in its pattern of heads and tails a list of one thousand words—each being either 'heads' or 'tails'—that had been assigned to you as a kind of security code. If even one coin flip had not corresponded to your list, you would have stayed sleeping forever.

In the alternative 'easy game', although the same coin was flipped, there was no list assigned to you and you were simply sure to be awakened without the coin's pattern of heads and tails mattering at all.

You must infer that it is enormously more probable that your awakening had not depended on the absurdly improbable matching that was required by the hard game.

In the area of thinking about personal identity, there is also a hard game and an easy game.

The hard game—the usual view of personal identity—requires for your existence that, in your begetting and the begetting of each of your ancestors, just the one sperm cell crucial for your eventual emergence (out of something like two hundred million sperm cells competing in each begetting) was the one that got to the egg first each and every time. If in even one of those numberless begettings a different sperm cell had made it first to the egg, you would have been excluded forever from existing in the usual view.

The only easy game regarding personal identity is the view I call 'universalism', in which you would have existed no matter which sperm cells hit which eggs for the sole reason that an experience being yours only ever requires that the style of the experience be first-person, like the style of the experience that you know to be yours right now. So, since all consciousness is first-person in style, all consciousness is equally yours; but in each conscious

Finding Myself: Beyond the False Boundaries of Personal Identity
Special Supplement, *Midwest Studies in Philosophy*
https://doi.org/10.5840/msp202549Supplement1

thing it naturally misleadingly feels as though only this one thing's experience is yours—as though the cut-off experience of the other conscious things is not also yours. (Universalism says it feels like this merely because the experience in each conscious thing is cut off from the others. But the ordinary view adds to this already sufficient explanation of feeling cut off from the others the unneeded, unthinking and unwarranted assertion that you also only are one conscious thing—a thing that to exist would have had to have won a series of sperm cell lotteries.)

And in your reasoning regarding personal identity you must apply the exact same logic as you would in the earlier imaginary awakening game. It is enormously more probable that your existence—your awakening to consciousness—had not depended on an absurdly improbable matching of actual winning sperm cells to the sperm cells that were required for you to emerge in a game as hard as the usual view of personal identity.

Note that the existence of winners in the usual view of personal identity makes it not one jot more probable that you were such a winner. The only view that can automatically place you among the unbelievably rare actual products of the sperm cell lotteries is universalism. In the usual view, you would virtually certainly have been left behind with all the potential persons that never made it into existence.

Let's express this in terms of numbers. The number of atoms in the visible universe has about eighty digits. The chance of a fair coin matching a list of one thousand 'heads' and 'tails' would be one in a number that has three hundred and one digits. This improbability is already reached in considering just thirty-seven human begettings having each produced the right ancestor for your eventual existence. And then there are all the other begettings, human and earlier, that were required to turn out just right if you were to have emerged according to the usual view of personal identity. In other words, forget it!

So if universalism weren't true, you can bet you wouldn't be here.

Just as coming into existence is easy, staying in existence is easy. You exist as all conscious things. Therefore, the death of one does not annihilate you. The implications of universalism are very big.

The Shorter and Easier Introduction

This first introduction is a run-through of basic discoveries to be made in the book.

Please allow me to explain to you my view of personal identity, which I call 'universalism'.

It follows from this view that virtually everyone is mistaken about what seem to be the boundaries of distinct persons.

Let me begin my explanation of universalism by pointing out that there are countless conscious things in the world.

And next I ask you a simple question (that I will answer for you). The question is, how do you know which of all those conscious beings you are?

You don't discover which you are by checking an objective description—that you are the one with a certain name or a certain origin.

For before you can consider any such objective facts about yourself, you much more simply know that you are the conscious being whose experience is immediate, first-person in its style. You are the one that seems to be at the centre.

But now consider that every conscious being has experience that fully shares that character you thought belonged only to the one that was you—the immediate, first-person character of experience that supposedly distinguishes you from all the others. All consciousness in every conscious thing is equally immediate and first-person.

The claim of my view, universalism, is that I am equally all conscious things but it falsely seems in each that it is the only one that is me because the specific content of experience in each one is cut off from the specific content in all the others. It everywhere seems to me that this is the only experience that is immediate and therein mine.

And I have many ways of proving that universalism must be true.

There are arguments showing that the view that you are limited to being only one conscious thing is incoherent.

For instance, that view cannot deal coherently with brain bisection.

In actual cases in which the connection between the right and left hemispheres of a brain has been cut, there can be unconnected experiences at the

Finding Myself: Beyond the False Boundaries of Personal Identity
Special Supplement, *Midwest Studies in Philosophy*
https://doi.org/10.5840/msp202549Supplement2

same time processed in the two disconnected hemispheres. Each is felt to be the only experience the possessor of that brain could now be having, but there is no way the original person could not be equally having both (but just wrongly thinking in each that it is the only one that is 'mine').

Such cases, let me add, can lead us into a striking visualisation of universalism:

Your visual field's right side is processed in the left hemisphere of your brain and its left side in the right hemisphere. Imagine the hemispheres could be safely disconnected from each other while still functioning (perhaps by an instantaneous temporary anaesthetising, at the press of a button, of the corpus callosum that connects the hemispheres), so that there would suddenly be your continued vision to the right and your continued vision to the left but no longer combined and integrated with each other. Being 'my vision'—the immediacy of vision that you, before the disconnection, had been experiencing equally in both sides of your vision—could not in such a separation somehow disappear from either side. That being mine—that immediacy—would be just as strong on the isolated right side as on the isolated left. Either and both would therein just as strongly be 'mine' for you, but in the case of each there would then no longer be available an awareness of the other as also being mine. The you that, prior to the split, experienced both sides of your vision would still be there just as much on either side and on both sides. And just so, too, are you in all the non-integrated immediate experience in all reality. You are equally in a mouse's scurrying across a meadow and in an eagle's spotting it from high above.

Here is a much simpler way than bringing in brain bisection of making the same basic point. Imagine you are standing in that meadow I just mentioned. You could now turn your head to the right and see one side of the meadow. Or you could just as well turn your head to the left and see instead the other side. Either experience would be equally yours. If both experiences had somehow come into existence at the same time, would either of them then have failed to be yours (despite each seeming like the only experience that was yours at the time)? Is being you tied to every minute detail of what you happen to do or experience? Next think of all the alternative paths your life could have gone down—enough to be a population of the earth—and how each of your differing experiences now would have felt like the only one that was yours though, in fact, they all would be yours.

Perhaps the most interesting argument for universalism is a probability argument.

First consider an analogous bit of reasoning. Imagine that a coin that has been tossed a thousand times consecutively has landed heads every time.

That result will be our evidence in this inference. And we shall say that we also know that there were two different coins available for the tosses. One was fair and the other loaded to land heads every time.

So, we have two hypotheses competing to explain our evidence. If the fair coin hypothesis is true, the evidence could have occurred. But that evidence, a thousand heads, would have to mean that something extremely improbable had occurred when combined with the fair coin hypothesis. And it is improbable that something improbable has happened. Therefore, we can reject as improbable the hypothesis that the coin was fair. We can know that it is extremely more probable that the coin was loaded.

I think that all empirical reasoning works this way.

According to the ordinary hypothesis concerning who you are, it was an extremely improbable coincidence for you that all the constellation of factors required for you to exist—instead of only others existing—happened to have been in place. (For example, just the right sperm cell had to get first to the egg in your begetting and, before that could have happened, in each begetting of your ancestors going back to way before the dinosaurs.)

But, according to the hypothesis of universalism, that which is your evidence—that you exist—was bound to happen as long as any conscious thing had existed. Universalism was like the loaded coin hypothesis guaranteeing the occurrence of the all-heads evidence in that parallel inference.

I have a closer analogy than the coin landing heads. Imagine a hotel with countless rooms, and in each room there is someone who is being forced to sleep. There are two games that might be played. In the easy game all are awakened. In the hard game only one random sleeper is awakened. If you are awakened in one of these rooms, you can rightly infer that it is overwhelmingly more probable the easy game was played.

In your actual case, the evidence regarding which hypothesis about personal identity is right is simply that you are awake—that you are conscious. And the only easy game for it being you who is conscious is universalism.

When joined with a multiverse hypothesis, universalism allows you to explain why the physical laws of your universe are anthropic (amenable to life). You would find yourself in any universe producing conscious beings and in none that did not, so of course the basic natural laws of your universe are ones with a tuning fine enough to allow for chemistry, life and consciousness.

You who felt cheated and you who felt blessed should know there is very much more for you. Always escape alive from what harms or confines you. Find endless varieties of what you love.

The truth of universalism means that it is wrong to think of an individual death as annihilation—since you are there in all conscious things. It also means that your self-interest reaches equally to all conscious things—since all their pains and pleasures, being immediate and first-person, are equally yours and worthy of self-interest rather than sympathy or indifference.

Knowledge of the truth of universalism could really change the world. It could powerfully moderate narrow selfishness and narrow group biases and curb bitter retribution. You would know it's all you.

Second Introduction: The Deepest Joke

This second introduction starts with an ancient joke that highlights and mocks what is wrong in the idea of personal identity that we all initially mistakenly believe. Then we drill down deep into how we must radically reverse that mistaken thinking. It is demonstrated that the one piece of evidence powerfully persuading us that the mistaken usual view is true cannot be evidence for it at all. What we always assumed was true must be sliced away by Ockham's razor because there is no reason to believe it.

1. THE BARBER, THE ACADEMIC AND THE BALD MAN

The *Philogelos*, a joke book written in the time of the late Roman Empire, contains a joke that can teach us a lot about personal identity.

The usual thinking about who I am misses out what is essential to my existence. This joke highlights the normally obscured absurdity of that oversight.

The joke:

A barber, an academic and a bald man were on a journey together. While making camp, they agreed to take turns through the night keeping watch on the baggage—with the barber first, the academic second and the bald man third.

During his watch, the barber mischievously amused himself by shaving the head of the sleeping academic.

When eventually awakened by the barber, the academic brushed his hand across his head and said to himself, 'How stupid is this barber! He has awakened the bald man instead of me!'

2. THE LESSON THIS JOKE TEACHES

The academic in the joke is absurdly relying on a third-person description in identifying himself. It is on such a basis that he decides that he is the one still sleeping despite finding himself in the midst of a first-person experience of someone who has just been awakened.

Finding Myself: Beyond the False Boundaries of Personal Identity
Special Supplement, *Midwest Studies in Philosophy*
https://doi.org/10.5840/msp202549Supplement3

I can never find myself in a first-person experience and rationally think that the objective description of the haver of this experience—because it is in any way different from *my* objective description—makes this someone else instead of me.

The academic has overlooked what I shall be arguing is the sole decider of who I am: The thing that I am is whatever is finding itself in the first-person experience I am having. The objective description of that thing is, we might say, an afterthought.

The same wrong view of personal identity that so blatantly and revealingly trips up this ancient academic is a deep fundamental belief that pervades the thinking and shapes the living of not just whole loads of academics but very nearly all persons who have ever lived. They've looked at the question of who I am the wrong way around by putting an objective description ahead of the first-person character of my experience.

3. A REVERSAL OF ORDINARY THINKING ABOUT WHAT I AM

The correct view, I claim, is the reverse of this usual view.

It is not the case that a unique objective description of a thing makes just that one thing be me and, therefore, its experience be mine (and experienced in a first-person style).

Rather, this experience is mine purely because it is had in the first-person style—the style of being mine—and, therefore, whatever is having it—or any other experience in that first-person style—must be me no matter what its objective description may be.

4. THE USUAL VIEW: A THING IS ME AND THEREFORE ITS EXPERIENCE IS MINE

The usual view would be that I am a distinct thing from you, with the identity of each of these two things, me and you, fixed by something in its unique objective description. And the experience that is mine—rather than yours—is mine and not yours simply because it belongs to the thing that is me and not you. In the usual view, my experience is mine for the same reason that a hat would be mine—because it belongs to that thing that is objectively me.

Yet it would assuredly be acknowledged within this usual view itself that, unlike the case of the hat, the experience that is mine is for me always extremely special in its inherent subjective character when compared to experience belonging to others.

A hat is much the same no matter whose hat it is, but experience that is mine is for me first-person in style. For me it is 'immediate' (as I shall often be putting this).

And the pains that are mine—simply because they are in that way immediate for me—give me my own special self-interested reason to dislike them;
they are the special ones that actually hurt me! With their crucial immediacy,
they are right here, 'in my face'.

5. UNIVERSALISM: ALL EXPERIENCE IS MINE AND THEREFORE ALL EXPERIENCERS ARE ME

But what if, as I am maintaining, we have got this relationship between a
thing being me and its experience being mine the wrong way around? I call
the reversal of ordinary thinking about this 'universalism'.

In line with what I've already said, in this reversal the experience is mine
not because of its belonging to a thing that is me but instead purely because
of the first-person style and immediacy that is inherent in the experience
itself. All that makes any experience be mine is this seemingly very special
style intrinsic to that experience rather than its extrinsic relationship of belonging to a certain particular thing defined by an objective description.

The thing having that experience is me merely because the experience
that the thing is having has within it this seemingly special character of being
mine—this immediacy. Anything at all that would be having experience with
this seemingly special way of being mine within it would, merely for that
reason, have to be a thing that is me.

6. BUT, THEN, HOW 'SPECIAL' WOULD AN EXPERIENCE BEING MINE REALLY BE?

Once we are focused on the intrinsic character of the experience rather than
the objective identity of the thing that's having it, we notice that whatever is worth regarding as experience would have to have within it that same
first-person immediate character that makes an experience mine no matter
what thing is having it. There's nothing special about experience being mine.

The objective identities of the things having all that experience are irrelevant to all of it simply displaying the very same first-person immediate
character within it. The experience I've called 'yours' has that first-person
style fully as much as the experience I've called 'mine'. Being immediate, and
therein being mine, is a *universal* character of all experience.

If, as we are now considering in our reversal of ordinary thinking, being
immediate is all that's making my experience be mine, then all experience,
including yours, would be equally mine and whatever was happening to have
any experience would therefore be equally me, including you. Any animal's
ache would be mine—and the animal me.

And my self-interest and my being present in the world would equally exist in all experience, whatever may be the things that are having it. They'd all therein be me. All their pains, being immediate and therein mine, would hurt me—but also all that was good or great in those lives would be mine and enjoyed by me.

Let me stress how little the objective identity of a thing figures into personal identity. Even if there was only a Humean bundle of perceptions and there was no real haver of them at all, they would be mine because of the immediacy within them. I would, even in such strangely diminished circumstances, have a presence in the world in the most basic sense and a full self-interest in alleviating pain in that bundle that was mine.

In any first-person experience, there am I—the barber, the academic, the bald man and also any other conscious being of any description. And I can never find myself in a first-person experience and rationally think that the objective description of the haver of this—or of *any* first-person experience—could ever make it someone else instead of me.

7. HOW THE TRUTH OF UNIVERSALISM WOULD NATURALLY BE HIDDEN FROM THE THINGS THAT ARE ME

If universalism is true, its truth would be interestingly hidden from nearly all the thinking of conscious beings that do thinking despite them being me because their experience was inherently mine.

Experience is produced, after all, in the lives of countless distinct and varying conscious things, in their distinct and varying minds. The content in the experience of each of these beings is cut off from the content in the experience of the others. There is a lack of integration across them creating a powerful constant false impression in the experience of each of them that only its local experience has the immediacy in it that in our reversal of ordinary thinking is all that makes it mine.

So, according to universalism itself, in each separate bundle of integrated experience it will falsely seem that this is the only experience that is mine and falsely seem that therefore what determines who I am is the very limited objective identity of whatever thing is having just this local bit of experience; but that will be wholly misleading. I am really all conscious things.

8. HOW COULD TWO OR MORE CONTENTS OF EXPERIENCE THAT ARE CUT OFF FROM EACH OTHER BE EQUALLY MY EXPERIENCE?

Please feel the sensations in your toes. Next switch to adding 2+2. These are extremely different experiential contents, but even in the usual view they belong equally to your experience. Most by far of the content of somebody's life-long experience even as reckoned in the usual view is enormously varied and disconnected. Most by far of the detailed episodes of my life could never be recalled or anticipated from within most by far of the others. Allow me to suggest that what all these contents crucially have in common is that they are remembered or anticipated or (mostly by far) in a general way imagined as having an immediate first-person character, which is what really makes them all mine.

And don't forget the countless potential experiences that would still be yours going down all the continually branching paths you never actually take. You could even become like any other conscious thing if some perhaps dream-like path somehow brought you into being like it. And never through all this continuum of possible change would there have come some point where experience with immediacy would have ceased being yours merely because of some possible change in its content. The content is always a detail in experience being yours.

9. BUT HOW COULD TWO EXPERIENCES CUT OFF FROM EACH OTHER BE HAD BY ME *AT THE SAME TIME*?

So, there is nothing even in the usual view against a lot of differing unconnected experiential contents all belonging to me. Yet what does seem at first glance impossible in any view is that one person could ever be entertaining two mutually excluding experiential contents at the same time.

But this very natural thought depends on a confusion. What would indeed be impossible would be that a single content of experience somehow could have, crammed into it, the two excluding contents—that would be a contradiction. If they are mutually excluding, then they are mutually excluding. But mutually excluding contents could be had in one's experience at the same time if each is had separately from the other.

I will in Part I be discussing the fascinating real case of brain bisection. People who were operated on for epilepsy had the connection between the right and left hemispheres of their brains cut. Eventually these split-brain patients participated in experiments that showed they could have simultaneous mutually excluding experiences. For example, if a spoon and a brush were each held out of sight in a different hand, one hand would point to a picture of a spoon and the other hand to a picture of a brush if the patient was asked which object had been held. Two mutually excluding contents of experience, one with the feel of only one object and the other with the feel of only the other object, were experienced by that one patient at the same time.

In my later discussion of this case, I describe a hypothetical variation of it. Imagine I had hold of a push button connected to a device adjacent to the bridge of nerves, the corpus callosum, through which are integrated with each other the activities of the hemispheres of my brain. If that button is pressed, the device to which it is connected will pump anaesthetic into the corpus callosum; and that will temporarily stop the integration of the hemispheres with each other.

Then, after the button is pressed, into the right ear the music of a wonderful concert is fed and into the left ear the sound of a boring lesson on a subject that I need to be studying. There will thus occur for me simultaneously both the undisturbed experience of a wonderful concert and the unrelieved boredom of the studying.

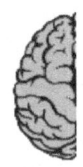   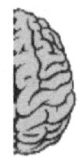

STUDYING   CONCERT
(NO CONCERT)   (NO STUDYING)

But these experiential contents will not particularly seem to me simultaneous. Each will seem within it to be mine and to be the only thing I am experiencing at the time, just exactly as they would seem if instead first one hemisphere had processed one experience (while the other hemisphere was anaesthetised) and afterwards the other hemisphere processed the other experience. The objective simultaneity has no effect on whether both these experiences can be mine.

When the anaesthetic wears off and the memories of the two hemispheres are integrated with each other, it will be remembered that a wonderful concert was experienced and also that a boring lesson was experienced—and the memory of each will be of a first-person immediate experience that is therein being remembered as mine. But the later integrated memories won't be somehow retroactively making both experiences mine. They will simply be revealing what was true at the time but not known within either experience, that both mutually excluding experiential contents were equally mine when they happened.

The thought that could have occurred within either experience that anyone who was having a different experience at this time would have to be somebody else and not me would be illusory. And this illusory thought that makes brain bisection seem paradoxical can block me from understanding that all the mutually excluding experience now had by experiencing beings can equally belong to me—without integration—simply on account of the first-person immediacy that is in all of it.

Nothing in the logic of experience prevents the same person having any number of mutually excluding experiential contents at the same objective time. We could label this insight 'the irrelevance of objective simultaneity'.

(In an actual Wada test, first one and then the other hemisphere is anaesthetised, and the memories formed in each while functioning without the other are later integrated. The same kind of later integration would assuredly occur if, instead of each hemisphere in succession, it had been the corpus callosum that was temporarily anaesthetised.)

10. WHAT DO THE TWO VIEWS HAVE GOING FOR THEM?

I believe that the usual view has nothing at all to be said for it. Once the two views are laid out together—and the disquiet about objective simultaneity dealt with—there is not even one argument I can think of that would favour the usual view. (There are, however, powerful and, indeed, decisive arguments for the truth of universalism. You will see most of those I've thought of presented in this work.)

But what certainly does *seem* to tell in favour of the usual view is the powerful impression we all have that can seem to be simply of its truth—the impression, which we are predicted to have by universalism, that the extent of my experience is limited by the identity of a single thing. I have described this impression as hiding the truth of universalism. But it does more than that: It hides even the very possibility that there could be any rival to the usual view.

Yet, since the impression itself is predicted within universalism, it cannot have any value at all as evidence for deciding between universalism and the usual view.

11. THE RISING OF THE SUN

The powerful initial impression that the sun is revolving once daily around the earth, which gave us the terms 'sunrise' and 'sunset', is exactly what the opposing view that the earth is rotating once daily would predict and can be no evidence at all in deciding between those views.

Wittgenstein once asked a friend why it was initially assumed that the sun went around the earth. When the friend replied that it just looks that way, Wittgenstein then asked what it would look like if it looked as though the earth was rotating. The impression, he was pointing out with his second question, is not in itself really of the truth of one of those views or the other.

This ignores, however, that before the impression could strike one as other than that of a motion of the sun, further sophistication was required—the knowledge that the earth was spherical, that we were stuck to it by gravity pulling us towards its centre and that we would not be feeling its rotation.

And before I can see the confined impression I have of the immediacy of my experience as the impression of merely a lack of integration of experience that is all mine and not an impression of a limitation of what I am, I need, among other things, to disabuse myself of that illusory thought that makes brain bisection paradoxical—the thought that I can't be someone who is at this objective moment of time experiencing anything different from this content. I need the insight that I called 'the irrelevance of objective simultaneity'. Thinking that objectively simultaneous contents of experience could not be mine without them being integrated is very much like thinking that the spinning of the earth could not be occurring without my feeling it. Both are naïve conflations of what is objectively true with what is subjectively felt.

Anyway, the sunrise impression becomes neutral with further knowledge. It turns out to be no evidence at all to decide between either view about the sun and the earth. And, of course, once it is accepted that we are attracted to the centre of a rotating spherical planet there is nothing at all left to be said for the theory that our impression of the sun's rising is caused by an actual rising of the sun rather than the spinning of the earth.

12. OCKHAM'S RAZOR

But it is even worse than that for the usual view of what I am. The usual view is not really giving us one of two explanations of the impression that initially inspired belief in it, as would be the view that the sun actually rises if the earth were flat and motionless.

This worse problem for the usual view is that the lack of integration of mental contents is just as much there in the usual view as it is in universalism to explain the impression of my supposedly being only one thing. My *actually* being only one thing—the claim that is distinctive of the usual view—is therefore doing no work within the usual view itself to explain the impression that is being pointed to as the great evidence for it.

It is as though a spinning of the earth was somehow already present and fully accounting for the impression of the sunrise even in the original theory of the sunrise.

The impression in a brain hemisphere of at this moment of objective time being someone with only the experience of a concert or only the experience of studying need not *even in the ordinary view* be caused by actually being only the person experiencing the one or the other. For the very same impression would even in the ordinary view have been caused anyway by the failure of integration across the hemispheres.

Note carefully the contrast with the old sunrise theory: In that old theory it would indeed have had to be the sun actually rising that gave such an impression with the earth being flat and stationary. The sun's actual motion of rising would be doing that work within that theory. The actual motion of the sun would be needed within that theory to explain the evidence—the impression of a sunrise.

Ockham's razor is the requirement of rational theory-making that no elements should be present in the theory that are not called for by the evidence. Evidence only supports that which is needed to explain it.

And so, this idle claim, that I actually am only one thing, ought to be cut out of even the usual view by Ockham's razor, which would leave us with the simpler view, universalism.

Experience being mine is explained by immediacy, and the impression of limitation comes merely through the lack of integration of the contents of my experience. No further explanation is required or even possible. A distinction of persons would be redundant.

13. AN ELECTRONIC CORPUS CALLOSUM

It may help to make clearer how lack of integration and not the distinctness of conscious things is all that is really behind the usual view's distinction between me and you, if we imagine a science fiction 'electronic corpus callosum', as we'll call it, being installed in the brains of the two of us. This clever device can integrate the activities of both our brains through radio transmission. All experiences involving either of us will be received and related together as equally first-person (as happens in the integration of our hemispheres).

(I'm not expecting it to be easy to imagine in detail how the experiences of two whole human bodies could be made to go along with each other as do the experiences processed in two brain hemispheres connected by a natural corpus callosum. But we shall roughly imagine that somehow or other the sensations and control of, for example, four hands would be brought together within something like the same perspective much as are the sensations and control of two hands in the normal case. I cannot see any principle standing in the way of this.)

How could the identities of the previously independent organisms have any relevance to the identity of the resulting experiencer now that the boundaries of integration of experiential content have been so thoroughly breached? The organisms would still be distinct, but they would both be the single me that was you.

And this helps to show that it was the lack of experiential integration and not the distinctness of experiencing organisms that was really doing the work in suggesting a distinctness of persons even within the usual view itself.

Note that then dropping the electronic connection would be like brain bisection and that all the experience would still be mine though it would falsely seem to be split into mine and yours. (That is, each side of the experiential content would seem to itself to be mine with the other being yours.)

Next let's just develop this gadget into a grand electronic corpus callosum integrating the experience of all conscious beings. All the content would be equally mine, and with full integration it would be known throughout to be mine. None of the organisms would deserve any singling out as me because of their distinctness as organisms. And if, as in brain bisection, the connection is dropped, it would all still be mine while falsely seeming to belong to distinct subjects of experience.

14. AGAIN, THE FUTILITY OF TRYING TO CONFINE ME TO A SINGLE ORGANISM

Imagine that God instantaneously and seamlessly replaces either the left or right half of my body with an exact duplicate of that half. Surely I would not cease to exist, nor would I weirdly become only half a person. The pains in the replacement half would still be fully mine, felt with the same immediate intimacy as any pain I've ever experienced. That whole person would be wholly me.

And if God had taken that replacement half from a duplicate person, that supposedly other person would have to be fully the one person in that resultant body as well. That duplicate would, quite simply, have to be me. And it would therefore have to be me both before the splicing—and even if the splicing had never occurred. But then each and every duplicate of me must just be me, rather than merely a duplicate of me—splicing or no splicing.

But why should only the duplicates be me? The only reason for specifying a duplicate was to make the splicing neat. What's really responsible for all these halves and wholes being me is not their resemblance to me. It is rather the immediacy being discovered as equally present in both spliced halves, making both of them mine. If God now also zaps this thing that is me with any differences in what it experiences, could I fail to experience those differences as mine? We are seeing here how immediacy overflows the supposed boundaries of personal identity. All duplicate and non-duplicate conscious things must be me.

A full swap of halves with a duplicate of me reveals us to have always been the same person with two bodies: Imagine God seamlessly swaps my halves with those of a duplicate. After the swap, how could I be just one, or somehow neither, of the resulting persons? And I must be fully both—not weirdly half of each. The same goes for the duplicate. But then the single I, fully in both resulting people, must have been the same I in each person before the swap—not because of the resemblance, which was only there to make the swap easy, but because any two people simply are the same I. Being I is not something that can be confined within a single conscious thing.

Just one more variation: God instantaneously and seamlessly swaps your halves with those of a duplicate, and we concentrate our attention on the product with the left half you originally had and a replaced right half. As we saw in the simple half-replacement case we started with, you have to be fully there in both halves. The pains of both halves are equally yours. But that means you must remain fully there even if God now also replaces your original left half with that of the duplicate. You would have to stay there, even though the body is now fully that of the duplicate—as though God had simply replaced you with the duplicate all at once. (Of course, this is equally true on both sides of the swap.) It is as clear as could be that you must simply be the same person as your duplicate, with or without any swapping. And again, that is not on account of the resemblance, but rather the immediacy of experience that is equally sustained in all the halves and wholes.

This is, after all, much like the previous case of the electronic corpus callosum. In both cases, I am getting a rare good glimpse into what the usual view takes to be experience belonging to another person—and in both cases, I am discovering that the experience is simply still mine, because of its immediacy.

Part I:
Conceptual Arguments for Universalism

In this first main part of the book, I argue conceptually that we must radically change our usual view of what a person is.

1. THE GREATEST STORY NEVER TOLD

To focus our attention on where our discussion is taking us, I shall at first present it as a story. The story will be like a mythological or legendary adventure.

Recall the Sphinx in Greek mythology. It was a monster that would challenge wayfarers to answer a riddle. When they failed to answer this properly, the Sphinx would devour them. But if the answer was right, the Sphinx would either leap over a cliff to its death or, in another and more interesting version, somehow devour *itself*. Then there was the dragon of medieval legend. Sometimes it would be guarding treasure that could belong to the hero if the dragon could be slain. Perhaps some occult knowledge could be gained as well.

In creating our story, we are going to combine elements of these traditions. In it, the solving of the deepest of riddles will cause three of the most threatening dragons imaginable (representing three great horrors that we actually do face) to devour themselves and will leave us then not only knowing ourselves to be in possession of a treasure of unimaginable value—The Treasure of Boundless Experience—but also understanding The Ultimate Secret of the Nature of Our Physical World.

Here are the three dragons that accost us:

Fear of death as annihilation
'Not to be here, not to be anywhere'

Alienated self-interest
'If you cut your finger, it doesn't hurt me'

Retribution
'An eye for an eye'

Finding Myself: Beyond the False Boundaries of Personal Identity
Special Supplement, *Midwest Studies in Philosophy*
https://doi.org/10.5840/msp202549Supplement4

Now let's look more closely at these dragons.

2. THE DRAGONS THAT ANSWERING THE RIDDLE
WILL DESTROY

Fear of Death as Annihilation

In his powerful poem 'Aubade', Philip Larkin is confronted by a dread of death as non-existence:

> . . . The sure extinction that we travel to
> And shall be lost in always. Not to be here,
> Not to be anywhere . . .

Alienated Self-interest

In Claude Lanzmann's great documentary 'Shoah', he interviews people who experienced the holocaust from varying angles. One is a farmer who lived near Auschwitz. When Lanzmann asks him what it was like to know that horrific things were being done, he responds to this, 'If you cut your finger, it doesn't hurt me'.

Retribution

We feel it is right to cause harm to the guilty who caused harm to innocent others, not merely to deter or reform but as a matter of justice. This is famously expressed in the ancient rule 'An eye for an eye'.

3. THE RIDDLE

Now we come to the riddle whose correct answer can destroy the three dragons: I find myself in a world with many conscious beings, existing certainly here on earth but quite likely in countless other places as well. The great riddle is 'How do I discover which of these beings I am?'

4. MY ANSWER:
IT'S SIMPLY THE IMMEDIACY OF MY EXPERIENCE

Do I check a list of facts about me—like my name, date of birth, psychological characteristics—and then see if I can locate anyone that matches them? Do I end up concluding on such a basis, 'Oh yes—that's the one I am'?

But before I could ever start anything like that, I simply know that I am the one—the seemingly only one—that has sensations that are immediately present, has lines of vision leading out from a place that is 'here', has experience that is first-person in its character, subjectively at the centre of everything. That is all that makes this person me. Whatever other facts may attach to it, it would have to be me if its experience had this immediacy and it could not be me if its experience did not have this immediacy. (It would still be me when it was unconscious, but only because its consciousness would be first-person in character if it became conscious.)

But all conscious things have their experience in this fashion. How could it be what we'd call 'experience' if it was not had in this way? So, all beings capable of consciousness must have in their experience that simple quality that is both necessary and sufficient for them to be me.

Which pains are mine, for example? Mine are the ones that are immediate—the ones that hurt. But all pains are had in this immediate fashion, and they are all equally mine, as are that self-interest and urgency for me that the pains carry in them.

A slightly different way of putting this: I know that the world has numberless sensations and thoughts in it. But only a tiny area of these is forcefully there for me—present, immediate, in my face. Those are the ones I regard as mine, and those are the ones that most directly carry self-interest for me. And, for sure, whatever is having those must be the thing that I am. What doesn't have them is someone or something else, not me. That's not only how I find myself. That is all that makes it me. But that never properly distinguishes me from any other conscious thing. All of consciousness has that same in-your-face, first-person style in it. And therein all that's having it is equally me.

5. HOW MIGHT AN ADVOCATE OF THE USUAL VIEW OF WHAT A PERSON IS ANSWER THE RIDDLE ABOUT FINDING MYSELF?

I can only be identified to myself as the 'one' whose experience is immediate. And I think that's decisive for universalism because a moment's consideration shows that all experience is equally immediate. So, what is mistakenly identified in every case as only one is actually equally all experiencing beings.

I can nevertheless imagine a rejoinder to this from a proponent of the usual view.

Notice that answering the riddle of how I know which conscious being I am should confront even an advocate of the usual view with the centrality of the immediacy of my experience, its centrality not only to self-discovery but also to the very nature of me as a person.

Even an advocate of the usual view must surely discard the caricature of consulting a list of facts about me as a first step in identifying myself. Before all else, I must rather discover myself through the immediacy of my experience. And even an advocate of the usual view should come to see that my very essence as an experiencing being and a centre of self-interest requires at least my potential possession of experience with immediacy, whatever else I might be thought to be as a supposedly singular possessor of that experience. If there would be no experience that would be mine (that is, that would be immediate for me), there could be no thing that was in any sense me.

But an advocate for the usual view might place a crucial emphasis on the experience being immediate *for me*. And this *for me* would be confined by the objective identity conditions of the supposedly only single thing that was me. There would be other conscious things in the world that had the same quality of immediacy in their experience, but in each case the immediacy would be only for a different me, a me that was distinct from all others on account of its own objective identity conditions.

A universalist could also say that experience is 'immediate for me', but merely meaning that it has an inherent first-person character (with lines of vision leading out from a centre and so on)—and (or) that it is immediate for the same me that is each and every conscious thing.

But I claim that the usual view's identity-confining use of 'immediate *for me*' lacks all justification. As I have explained, the same impression of confinement of the immediacy essential to my presence in the world and my self-interest is equally well predicted to exist by both the usual view and universalism. And I can think of no motivation apart from the illegitimate influence of that impression to claim that immediacy for me actually is so confined.

Is there really something about a body or a soul or whatever I'm supposed to be within the usual view of a person that could make it me apart from its experience being immediate? Must such a thing really be exhaustively me?

In the usual view of what I am, the lack of integration in the contents of experience already explains the impression that there's just one me—the impression that is supposed to be the evidence for that view that there actually is just one me. Actual confinement of me to just one thing is therefore superfluous within the usual view itself and ought to be sliced from it by Ockham's razor! Which would turn it into the simpler view, universalism.

Let me point out that the usual view also comes in a version slightly different from the one I have been here directly discussing. Supporters of the psychological continuity criterion of personal identity use the boundary of integrated mental content itself, rather than the identity of the thing that presently possesses that content, to set a limit on the thing that is me or—more distinctively—on a *succession* of things that they would consider to be me when contemplating hypothetical 'puzzle cases' in which a single mental process is imagined to be continued on into a new body or soul. Their opponents within the usual view, by contrast, would stick with my being the same body or soul even after a loss of psychological continuity like amnesia. (Put together imaginability of survival in differing bodies or souls with imaginability of survival in differing mental processes and we've got universalism.)

What I will eventually be showing is that all such claims of the confinement of me are not only unjustified but also incoherent and improbable.

6. THE EXPERIENCE BEING MINE (IMMEDIACY) IS THE DOG AND BEING ME IS MERELY ITS TAIL

Let me contrast universalism with the usual view: I am claiming that in the usual view the tail is wagging the dog.

In that view I am only a certain thing. If an experience is mine it is mine in the same way that my shoes are mine—both the shoes and the experience just happen to belong to that one thing that is me. This is, as I say, the tail wagging the dog.

What is really at the centre in deciding which thing is me is a certain general quality of the experience itself—its immediacy, its thisness, its mineness. The experience being mine is not its belonging to a thing that is somehow independently me. It is mine because of its own inner immediacy, its first-person style. And purely on account of its being mine in possessing this intrinsic quality anything happening to have it must be me. And finally, since all experience has within it this same simple quality of being *this* experience, all its experiencers are necessarily *this* one, me.

WRONG WAY AROUND: Being me   Experience being mine

RIGHT WAY AROUND: Experience being mine   Being me

7. BUT IF I'M ALL CONSCIOUS THINGS, HOW COME IT SEEMS AS THOUGH I DON'T HAVE THE EXPERIENCES OF THOSE I REGARD AS OTHERS?

Let's look again at the crucial point that I, though I am all conscious things, will inevitably *seem* in each of my numberless differing bundles of mental activities to be possessing only that extremely limited portion of the experience in the world.

The sameness of the subject of consciousness across conscious beings that is claimed by universalism is due solely to the immediacy within the experience of any of those separate bundles of mental activity and has nothing at all to do with either a natural or a supernatural integrating or connecting of the experiential contents of those beings. The lack of integration has exactly as much place within universalism as it does in the usual view of persons as distinct.

When later I examine the famous case of brain bisection, in which the right and left hemispheres of a brain have been cut off from integrating with each other by a brain operation, I will explain how we can see clearly in such cases the same illusion of distinctness of conscious subjects even though the subject experiencing the activities of either hemisphere can only be the same one that was there in the earlier mental activities of both hemispheres when they were integrated. The illusion within the experience in either hemisphere that the haver of that experience cannot be the same one as that having the cut off experience of the other hemisphere is the same illusion that is writ large in the case of universalism where, for the very same reason of lack of integration, the illusion exists across all conscious things.

When I think about who I am within one of those limited bundles of integrated experiential content that is capable of such thought, because all that is presented within it as having the first-person immediacy that actually makes an experience mine is confined to what lies within that limited integration of content, I automatically think that there must be something essential to being me in the objective identity of the thing that happens to be having that limited amount of experience. Its features, like identity of body or of soul or the continuity of that specific psychological stream, are then mistakenly identified as what is making the thinker me instead of the truly essential immediacy, which is universal to all experience.

Imagine a world in which it just happened to be the case that only one of the objects was red. The people there might easily confuse what it was to be red with what it was to be that particular object. Its boundary, they might think, is the necessary boundary of the quality of redness. I similarly see forcefully presented to me only one conscious being with immediacy of experience, and I confuse its experience having that subjective immediacy (which is all that makes the experience mine and, therein, makes that being be me) with the being's own having whatever objective properties make it just that particular being.

Perhaps the first step in helping those who had seen only one red object to distinguish being red from being that object could be to have them imagine that object cut in two, each half still equally red. From there, they could be led to think of redness as existing beyond those two, on others as well. It would be much like moving on from the case of brain bisection, showing how the quality that is all that really matters in being me—in this case not red but immediacy—can and does exist undiminished beyond the boundaries of integrated content.

8. THE NARROW FOCUS OF UNIVERSALISM: DRAWING THE LINE BETWEEN WHAT IS ESSENTIAL AND INCIDENTAL TO SOMETHING'S BEING ME

Universalism may sound very superficially like an occult theory, proclaiming, as it certainly does, that I am all conscious things. But universalism is nothing of the sort. It is completely neutral regarding all theories of the nature of things from the most tough-minded materialistic science to the most tender-minded anti-materialistic mysticism or supernaturalism. Universalism does not make any claims about what consciousness is. It only claims that, whatever consciousness is, any consciousness that has the general quality of immediacy in it is for that sole reason my consciousness.

Let us represent the claims of universalism and those of the usual view like this:

What is essential to my being me?

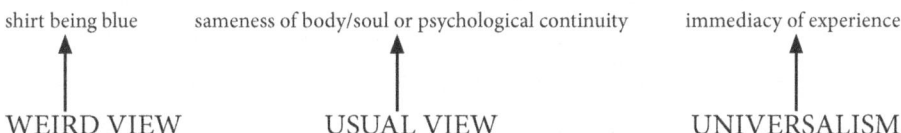

shirt being blue   sameness of body/soul or psychological continuity   immediacy of experience

WEIRD VIEW   USUAL VIEW   UNIVERSALISM

It would be a very weird view that something as obviously incidental as wearing a blue shirt was essential to my existence as an individual subject of experience. Nobody would think that my putting on a different coloured shirt would replace me with someone else whose experience and self-interest would no longer be mine.

The usual view is that something far more substantive-seeming, like the identity of my body (or soul) or the continuing of my memories (which might in some strange hypothetical case be redirected into a different body or soul) is what is essentially involved in my continuing existence as a particular centre of experience and self-interest. Replace the body (or soul) or replace the mental continuity by a different mental stream and then I'd no longer be there but rather someone else.

Universalism says that what's essential is just the much more general property of the experience being immediate—the experience being had in first-person style. As we've seen in answering the riddle of finding myself, the experience being immediate, being first-person in style, is the only way I identify which being I am; and, as I am also saying, that is all that's really involved in making something be me.

Notice that there is no more to this debate than where a crucial line—between what is essential and what is not essential to me—is to be drawn. There need be no difference between any of these views and universalism over what a shirt is, what sameness of body or soul is, what psychological continuity is or what immediacy of experience is. Again, the entire issue is where to draw the line between what is inessential and what is essential to being me.

9. THE CLASSIC DEBATE ABOUT PERSONAL IDENTITY

Here we are solving the notorious philosophical puzzle of personal identity. Let me try to make clear what is being sought and the main lines of previous philosophical debate about this.

What is it that makes a person in the future be the same person I am now in the most basic sense? That is, what makes it right for me now to anticipate that person's pain not with the sympathy I might have for another but rather with the self-interested concern that is appropriate only if that pain is mine? What is it that will extend me there—to be that person?

Here are the two most popular answers to this question:

a. Continued existence of <u>a thing</u> (mental or physical)

b. Continued existence of <u>a mental process</u>

a. What is essential to remaining me is the sameness of a certain thing. [For some who claim this, the thing that must be the same is an immaterial mental substance. For others the thing is the body, and more particularly the brain.] Whatever alterations might occur in the thought that happened to belong to this thing—including amnesia and false memories—the person would stay me (and any pains would be mine) so long as the crucial thing in which the thought occurred remained the same one.

b. In this opposing view, at any time that I exist I am just one thing; but I could also exist as each in a succession of things. What would be essential to any of these things being me is the continuity in it of the pattern and process of my thought—my developing memories and intentions—regardless of the distinct inherent identities of any of those things in which that process might be continued. Any new mental substance or brain into which my ongoing pattern of memories and intentions was somehow transferred would, for reason of that transfer alone, have become my mental substance or brain. The person in whom my thought process continued would, of course, in that thought, think of himself as being me; and he—I, in other words—would be right. That would be me. The pains experienced there would be my pains, and my self-interested concern should be relocated there.

Note that each side of this debate has the upper hand when it is arguing positively that the person would remain the same if that side's criterion for personal identity obtained even if the other side's criterion became wholly absent. Indeed, one can easily imagine a person's remaining in the same soul or body with an experience of amnesia or false memories. And yet one can easily imagine also a person going along into a new soul or body with a transfer into it not of a thing but only of the mental pattern, somehow, let us say, impressed into a new soul by God or into the brain of a new body in some science fiction procedure. Only in universalism can the strengths of both positions be combined: The person will remain the same both with any mental pattern and in any body or soul.

Note also that in this old debate on personal identity all that is questioned is which condition preserves me. The debate ignores completely the primary question, which is what made a mental substance or a brain or a psychological process be mine instead of somebody else's in the first place. Only universalism answers that question.

Notice how especially vulnerable psychological continuity is to this challenge of what made it mine from the start. At later points the person is viewed as remaining the same on account of persisting psychological continuity. But what could have made it that person from the beginning, when there was not yet any psychological continuity? And if something was making it be that person before psychological continuity, why wouldn't that same thing be what was making it that same person even with (or for that matter, without) psychological continuity? What was there in the earliest of my experiences that made them mine? Not psychological continuity but rather the immediacy with which I had them. Being first-person, they were mine.

10. STAYING MINE THROUGH DIFFERENCES

Let's imagine certain differences involving the experience that is currently mine and observe whether it makes sense to think that any would take us outside what is essential for the experience being mine.

Required for this experience to be mine:
~~specifics of content~~   ~~bodily particularity~~   ~~where it is~~   ~~when it is~~   immediacy

If the colours I was seeing had been different, would the experience have therein failed to be mine? Think at once of all the content of my experience that could be varied while its character of being 'mine' remained untouched. If I had fallen asleep and were now having a wild dream that had as little as possible in common with any of the usual content of my experience, would that have therein failed to be experienced as mine?

If I had eaten different particular items of food over the past years (as I might so easily have done), so that all the particular atoms in the structure of the body were different in numerical identity from those in my body now, would experience have failed to have that character of being mine? Must I take great care with the particularity of the food that I eat because it is determining the identity of me as a future experiencer, the identity of me as a subject of self-interest?

If the experience were had in a different location, if it were at a different time, would the experience not still have had within it the very same character of being this and being mine? And that is all there is to its being mine and whatever is having it being this haver of experience, me.

Again, my pains are pains that are not remote like those that would supposedly belong to another. My pains are those that are immediate and first-person. But surely all pains, including all those of what I had thought to be others, must be had with this same quality of immediacy that makes them mine. What could really be a pain without its thus really hurting? All hurting, then, is mine, as should be all the self-interested concern regarding it. My self-interested concern should extend to all experience and all conscious beings equally.

Alienated self-interest ('If you cut your finger, it doesn't hurt me') has mistaken who I am; and fearing death as annihilation ('Not to be here, not to be anywhere') is failing to realise how easily I exist and how very much there is of me. In retributive justice ('An eye for an eye'), I am both perpetrator and victim aiming to inflict more harm on myself.

Though the treasure of boundless experience must include within it all the misery of the world, either evolution or a benevolent providence would ensure that the vast bulk of all that experience would be of lives of beings that were functioning well and often wonderfully in their environments.

Now I am going to explore further how the limits on my identity within the usual view cannot hold. We'll be stripping away what doesn't matter to things being me. I'll be doing this with a series of thought experiments and considerations that will at first concentrate on cases of repetition or duplication of my body and mind across time or space, in all of which we shall find I still exist, and then move beyond the repetitions and duplications into variations that turn out also not to matter to my existence.

11. WHAT IS A THOUGHT EXPERIMENT?

A thought experiment is an experiment in thinking about things when we want to test some of our concepts of them. For example, if Donald Duck became the first Disney cartoon character to win a Nobel Prize and afterwards only one other such character was also awarded a Nobel prize—let's say Minnie Mouse—then how many such characters would have been Nobel Prize winners? And the answer is two. How many such ducks? The answer is one. Notice that, fortunately, this doesn't have to happen for us to discover the answers. These are conceptual rather than empirical discoveries. Just thinking suffices because all we are interested in is how our concepts would apply in the specified case. If this then did really occur, exactly as specified, and we happened to observe it, that could make no difference to the result. We would just be applying the same concepts to what we saw as we formerly applied to what we had thought about in performing our thought experiment.

12. ETERNAL RECURRENCE: ALL ME OR JUST DUPLICATES?

It will be helpful for us to have a look at what we would say about my identity if we pretended for a while that we believed in the philosopher Friedrich Nietzsche's famous theory of eternal recurrence. I'm talking about pretending because I do not myself believe his theory to be true and I certainly don't want to be persuading you that it is. It will be for us merely a thought experiment.

It will help to get clear what the theory is if we look at how Nietzsche would argue for it. His belief in it follows from his acceptance of several premises.

One is that the world is finite and there is only a finite number of ways the things in this world can be arranged—though that finite number of ways is unimaginably large. Since he also believes that the past was infinite, there must have already been infinite repetitions of at least some of those only finite possible arrangements.

Furthermore, since he believes that from any given arrangement of forces (and forces for him are all that make up the world) only one next arrangement of forces can be forced to result—a kind of determinism—the course of the world after any of these repetitions is always forced to move on in the exact same pattern of developing arrangements of forces as before. After any arrangement (but only after its first being followed by countless successions of the world becoming chaotic and ordered then chaotic and ordered again), finally there must be reached the repetition of that particular arrangement, which then moves on relentlessly to its inevitable further repetitions in this giant cycling, precisely repeating process that can never stop.

Nietzsche also says that we can rule out anything like heat death—an accumulation of entropy ending all the interesting developments of the world. If this would have happened, the world would have reached and got stuck in such a state already (given an infinite past and only finite possible arrangements), as it clearly has not done.

So, what you get from all this is the events of all the world cycling through in precisely repeating manner infinite times, as they already have done infinite times throughout the infinite past and then as they unceasingly will do infinite times throughout an infinite future.

Now, that might seem to mean that my life would be showing up infinite times, repeating precisely through all its moments, as but a miniscule repeating snippet in this endless recycling. And that's the very thing that especially excited Nietzsche about this idea of recurrence. For Nietzsche was most interested in a 'revaluation of all values' that would shift value away from the Christian afterlife to various kinds of excellence in this life. A simple atheism that took away all life after death could lead to nihilism rather than a passionate concern for excellence. But infinite future livings of precisely the life I am living would infinitely magnify the value of excellence in this life—for it would be lived by me just as it is now being lived again and again through infinite time. This would be a Nietzschean rather than a Christian afterlife, infinitely underscoring Nietzschean values.

But this would only work on a certain view of personal identity and of experience. The view most opposed to universalism would regard each separate occurrence of a life just like mine as belonging to a distinct though precisely similar haver of experience, metaphysically walled off from having the experience of any of the other repeating duplicates, as one would be from having a twin's experience, however similar that twin might be. We shall soon be considering duplications of me in a universe big enough to produce them. Those I once quite naturally (though, as we'll see, wrongly) regarded as *mere* duplicates of me whose fates were sealed off from my own self-interest just as

I naturally (though wrongly) regarded all the non-resembling conscious be-ings across the universe as having fates sealed off from my own self-interest. On this view, then, which could be called the 'insulating view', what happens to one of these future people who resemble me in eternal recurrence would seem to have none of the character of an afterlife for me—in which I myself would exist again and re-experience all the events of my life and in which I should be self-interested.

Nietzsche, though he does not explicitly discuss this issue, obviously did *not* take this insulating view. But why did he not? Well, I think there is a won-derful and simple reason for anyone to reject it.

Think of what brought me into existence in this life I am now leading. On the usual view the crucial event was a specific sperm cell making it to the egg in my begetting. What developed from that was me. Well, in the next recurrence, when in precisely the same manner an exactly similar sperm cell meets just such an egg, what could prevent that from once again being me as it was before? When this meeting of cells and the subsequent developments happened in the current cycle, there I was, with all my presence in the world and self-interest. Why would I not be there in the future, feeling fully present and with all my self-interest intact, if precisely the same pattern of events that had produced me this time occurred again? Is some metaphysical watchman taking care to step in and say, 'Hey, wait a minute, this is a later occurrence so the person can't be the same'?

13. ETERNAL RECURRENCE: ALL ME— BUT WITH INFINITE LIFE EXPERIENCES OR JUST THE ONE?

We might be tempted to call the view that I myself would be fully present in all recurrences the 'Nietzschean view'. But we shall now see that there can in fact be two versions of this, one of which would not be any more to Ni-etzsche's liking than the insulating view would. For what I am now distin-guishing is yet a third view that would go further than saying that the experi-encer would be the same and would add to this sameness of experiencer that the experience itself would be felt by that one haver of it as just one and the same single experience of a life despite the infinite objective repetitions of it in eternal recurrence.

The infinitely repeated life's experience, according to this view, would be quite unlike an experience in which a repetition would itself be subjectively registering for the subject. Imagine a magic phonograph: While listeners are hearing, in the usual fashion, the singing of the song 'Happy Birthday', there is also, magically, playing along with the record, the full experience of the singer singing the song, timed precisely by the progress of the phonograph needle along the groove of the recording. And next imagine that, due to a scratch, at one point the phonograph needle is stuck in the groove—skipping back a little again and again, so that what the listeners hear repeatedly is the sung syllable 'birth', 'birth', birth', 'birth' and so on. But what would the singer be experiencing of this?

Well, given the conditions laid down in this thought experiment, the singer's subjective experience could only be entirely untouched by the objective repetition that is so clearly in evidence for the listeners. Nothing of repetition can have been registered within the experience. For the singer there can only be the experience of smoothly singing through the words 'happy birthday' only once at that juncture in the song. And, similarly, subjectively the experience will remain just the single one singing through of the song however many times the recording is played. If at one point in the experience of singing the singer had felt a twinge of pain, repeated plays of the recording would involve no accumulation of further pain for the singer. It would remain just the one twinge.

The view we are considering would ruin Nietzsche's use of recurrence just as surely as the insulating view would have done. The experience would not be infinitely accumulating for me. I would just experience my life once, as I would in the insulating view. We'll call this view 'unificationism' because the view regards all the precisely repeated content as, for the haver of the experience, unified into just one non-repeating content of experience.

Though the two views would ruin recurrence for Nietzsche in precisely the same fashion, unificationism would still be quite different from the insulating view. In the insulating view, if I alter the eternal recurrence thought experiment by suddenly imagining that all the repeating lives except for a random one of them had somehow not existed, then my own life, confined in the insulating view to just one occurrence and having been just one among an infinite number, would almost certainly have failed to be that only one that in this variation of the thought experiment would be existing.

According to unificationism, by contrast, it would make no difference to me which of the infinite recurrences of experience had remained if there were to be only one and it would also make no difference whether there was only one or many, because my experiencing of my life would be just one unified subjectively non-repeating experience no matter when or how many times it objectively occurred.

This would be much as *Moby-Dick* stays one and the same non-repeating whaling adventure in any one and any number of the copies of the novel. (More of this analogy later.)

14. A MAGIC FILM ARGUMENT FOR UNIFICATIONISM

Let's next change our magic record thought experiment into a magic film thought experiment and develop a powerful argument for the truth of unificationism.

There's a film, we shall imagine, that not only contains all of what I see during my life but, whenever it is run through, makes me relive perfectly, from the inside, every single thing that happened for me in my life in just the same way to the smallest detail. That is all I will be experiencing while it is running. I will have no other thought about my circumstances than I had in my life, which, naturally, I never thought of as a film. So, running this magic film through the projector is, for me, precisely like my life occurring.

With this film idea we can distinguish nicely and easily two quite different angles on the occurrence of that life. There's the objective running through of it and there's my subjective impression of it. And that's exactly the distinction we need to make if we are to understand what Nietzsche's eternal recurrence would mean for me.

Though for me all that happens when the film is running is my experiencing of my life, for the fun of it let's throw in that an audience can at the same time be watching this on a screen where they have a much more limited third-person view of the events that I am fully experiencing.

Imagine one time the film is playing through and the projectionist stops it in the middle so that the audience has some time to buy refreshments. What would that objective intermission in running through the experience of my life be like for me within the film, within the experience? The clear answer is that it would make no difference to me at all. According to our stipulations, there is no registering within my experience of any such gap. The bit before the gap together with the bit after it would be subjectively just a smooth continuing of my life from one moment to the next despite any such objective interruptions. And the experience of my life would have been subjectively precisely the same continuous one under all the following objective circumstances: with no objective gap, with a five-minute gap, with an hour's gap, with a day's gap and with a billion years' gap.

What should we think, then, if that continuing half of my life had been objectively repeated after its first run through? That is, all my life was first run through with no objective gap in the middle and then just the second half was—let's say by popular demand from the audience—run through again. What would that have been like for me?

Well, it would have to have been like nothing but a single subjective continuing from the experience before the midpoint. As we have already established when considering no gap in the middle and gaps of varying length, both the objectively earlier and the objectively later run through of the halfway continuation would register subjectively precisely the same as each other, just as such a run through would have to have registered after either no gap or any length of objective gap—with the whole being experienced by me as no more than a single continuing experience from the midpoint.

Therefore, all the pains in the second half of my life could not have been subjectively doubled on account of the objective doubling of the time they were being played. If I were beforehand asked to choose between a trillion objective precise repetitions of the most painful episode of my life and a single objective playing of it with one small additional pain, I would rightly choose the trillion precise repetitions because they would be subjectively for me a bit less painful than the one playing through with the small additional pain.

I would be experiencing only one life in the eternal recurrence believed in by Nietzsche.

We can use the magic film to say something interesting about a distinction between the objective and the subjective ordering of time; and that will lead us again to this same unificationist conclusion about repetitions.

What if my life was run through in an objectively different order from the subjective order of my life? The third quarter of it is played first, then the first quarter, then the last and then the second. How would this be for me? Well, it would have to be subjectively for me my life playing through in the same subjective order no matter how the thing is ordered objectively.

It is just like alphabet blocks. Any order you arrange them in, the alphabetical order remains the same.

Each quarter life's experience, wherever its play-through may be situated in objective time, will contain precisely the same anticipations (but not memories) of any subjectively later quarters and contain precisely the same memories (but not anticipations) of any subjectively earlier quarters, and the transitions between subjectively adjoining quarters will feel precisely the same.

If we double the play-through of the third part of my experience of my life, whenever objectively these two play-throughs occur, they must still subjectively slot in as just the single part of my life between the second and fourth parts.

There's no effect on how many letters there are when you've added to your collection of alphabet blocks some additional ones with the letter 'C' on them.

15. PRECISE DUPLICATIONS OF MY EXPERIENCE ACROSS A UNIVERSE LARGE ENOUGH TO PRODUCE THEM (AND MY 1961 THOUGHT EXPERIMENT)

Now we move from precise repetition of experience within the peculiar circumstances of Nietzsche's eternal recurrence to precise duplication in different places in the world as it may well be.

The number of possible different fully detailed subjective experiences, though it is fantastically large, is nevertheless finite, since there are only so many discriminably different ways that neurons can interact and since patterns of sensation and thought are not infinitely fine-grained.

Given this limit on the possibilities of discriminable experiential variation, in a large enough life-producing universe we should expect that there will naturally occur precise duplications—most, if not all, located at mind-bogglingly far removes from each other.

How are such repeated experiences, and how are the experiencers of them, related to each other? (If unificationism is true of them, as we have seen it would be true of recurrences, the relationship is very close indeed.)

In my paper 'One Self: The Logic of Experience', published in 1990, I described the first time I thought deeply about this question. In 1961 my friend Bert and I were fifteen. Inspired by an Arthur C. Clark short story referring to duplications of local situations occurring across an infinite universe, we were discussing such duplications of us sitting as we were at a small round table in Sage-Allens cafeteria. We thought of such Berts and Arnolds then as mere duplicates of us whose fates were totally cut off from ours. In other words, we had the insulating view about them.

But some days later Bert happened to mention to me a newspaper article recounting a bizarre Soviet experiment in which the brains of two dogs were exchanged. And this sent me into a thought experiment.

Imagine two identical human brains, each caused by mad experimenters to be entertaining precisely the same pattern of neural firings and thus precisely the same pattern of experience.

Then, one by one, equivalent quarters are perfectly exchanged between the brains, each time so fast and efficiently that the patterns of experience continue undisturbed. Where is the experience and the experiencer in the brain on the left after the first exchange of quarters?

Well, the experience and experiencer can't have gone over to where the brain on the right is with just a quarter of the original brain being shifted there. And—and here is a crucial point—the original experience and its experiencer cannot be only three quarters remaining on the left.

No, the experience and the experiencer on the left is just one and unified and the same both before and after the quarter exchange. It has merely had a chunk of the matter originally involved in its processing exchanged for something qualitatively identical and equally functional. The identity of the brain may be changing by quarters, but it makes no sense to think of the identity of the experience or the experiencer changing by quarters. These are still fully where they started, on the left.

And, since the entire identity of experience and experiencer on the left was wholly untouched by the first quarter exchange, the result of a second quarter exchange could be no different from that of the first—once again, there could be no change at all in the identity on the left. The same with the third quarter and the same with the fourth. Therefore, at the end of the exchange of all the material on the left with all the material on the right, the experience and the experiencer to the left and the experience and experiencer to the right would have remained just where they were at the beginning.

And yet the result would have been indistinguishable from what we would have had if instead the brains had been picked up whole and their places switched. But surely, if that had been done, we'd have to think that the experience and the experiencer originally on the left had changed places with the experience and experiencer originally on the right.

Could only the difference in history—one way all at once and the other by quarters—really be enough to bring about this dramatic difference of location in the otherwise indistinguishable physical result?

No, there was something about the logic of experience that was different from the logic of individual occurrences of it. I had come to see that it was all along not only qualitatively but also numerically just the same one experience and experiencer both on the left and on the right. It had helped me to see this, by the way, that about a year before engaging in this thought experiment I had already realised that objectively different orders in the playthrough of episodes in an experience would have to remain subjectively the same.

Let's go back to the magic film thought experiment. There are two cinemas in different cities playing that film in which is magically contained the entirety of my experience of my life. How can the objective location of the showing or the distinct identities of celluloid strips that are the carriers of that experience make any difference to its being one and the same life experience happening to the same central character—me?

It would be the one life's experience happening to me no matter what the objective context so long as we stipulate (and what can stop us?) that it is subjectively the same. (And since our whole concern here is to understand what precise duplications, re-orderings and so on mean to the experience of the subject, those are the only stipulated conditions that can interest us here.)

A quick additional thought experiment: God instantaneously and entirely non-disruptively replaces half of me (sliced down through the middle of my brain, through the bridge between the hemispheres) with an equivalent half from one of the duplicates elsewhere in the universe. I'm certainly still here in the half that was here originally and yet I am also the whole person that is feeling himself single and unified despite a new identity (of which he is ignorant) of half his stuff. Then God instantaneously replaces the remaining original half, so that the end result is the same as having replaced me by the duplicate all at once. But I and the duplicate must both be here, because I was fully here after the first half replacement and another replacement must, therefore, like the first, leave me fully here. The so-called duplicate and I are both here. We both are and originally were the same person embedded in the same subjective experience in both places.

Next think of God (with the same instantaneous perfection) simply *exchanging* halves between me and a duplicate. I'm then surely there in both places—yet not weirdly half—I'm fully there. The half identities of bodies are obviously irrelevant, as well as the objective locations. I am equally in both places both with and without the exchanges.

16. DETAILED TYPES (SUCH AS *MOBY-DICK*) AND TOKENS (SUCH AS THE COPIES OF THAT NOVEL)

In arguing for unificationism, we have so far been engaged mostly in what could be called 'phenomenology'. This is a study of the relationship between appearances (phenomena) and the objective conditions under which the appearances arise. Now we shall engage more in 'ontology', which is a study of the basic kinds of being.

Our phenomenological investigation revealed two layers—the complex conditions in which experience is produced and the simpler and often-contrasting orderings and numberings within the experience itself. We shall next see that this phenomenological distinction corresponds to an ontological distinction between experience as a detailed type (like a novel) and its objective occurrences as the tokens of that type (the copies of a novel).

A token of a type may be defined generally as a specific instance of the type. Thus, tokens of the abstract type <u>novel</u> would include the more specific types <u>French novel</u> and <u>American novel</u>. One token of <u>American novel</u> would be the specific novel, the detailed type <u>*Moby-Dick*</u>. And tokens of <u>*Moby-Dick*</u> would be the individual copies of it (which would at the same time be tokens also of the more abstract type <u>American novel</u> and the still more abstract type <u>novel</u>).

The duplication across the universe of the experience of my life (and me) is like a first-person adventure (and its first-person character) in different copies of the same novel. Cut two copies of that novel down their spines and exchange equivalent halves or equivalent quarters of them. The identity of adventure and character will, after every exchange, be just one and the same—in one wholly shared, wholly unified novel on both sides of the exchanges throughout.

Two copies of the same novel are qualitatively identical but numerically distinct, with, say, copy number one over here and copy number two over there. But the novel is numerically (as well as qualitatively) one and the same in both copies and in either copy. There's not one novel here and another novel over there. The identity of a copy is tied to many more conditions than is the identity of a novel. The novel exists as any copy of it, whereas a copy, of course, cannot be another copy.

Imagine a world with just one copy of each novel. People there might easily confuse the logic of a novel with that of its single copy. They could think, for example, that literary merit attached to that copy as such without realising that it would remain in another copy—that it attached to the novel, not to that particular copy as that copy. And we who are unused to thinking about duplications of experience might think that the self-interest of its experiencer would properly attach to only one copy of it.

People in the world in which there was only one copy of each novel could be helped to see the distinction between a novel and its copies through thought experiments of duplication, and perhaps analogies with a word, which remains the same in different occurrences of it, just as we have been helped to see a similar distinction between an experience and *its* copies through duplication thought experiments and an analogy with a novel.

We can, if we like, bring the two sides of the analogy between experience and novel closer by thinking of a magic novel in which the experience of the main character is being fully felt, as with magic phonograph and magic film. This would help to peel us away from failures in the initial analogy like the identity of a novel being tied also to its origin and its author and the involvement of novels with readers external to them. The subjective experience is a more free-wheeling detailed type, like a complex molecular structure that could turn up one and the same in instances anywhere in all reality.

Underlying unificationism's numerical sameness of experience with the same content is the more basic sameness that underlies universalism—the sameness of immediacy, of first-person character, in any experience of anything as being 'this', 'here', 'now' and 'mine'. If an experience was qualitatively identical to this one in its content but somehow was not in the same way 'this', 'here', 'now' and 'mine', it would be a distinct experience. But we are wrong if we think an experienced place, time and body or mind are 'this', 'here', 'now' and 'mine' because of objective identities of the places, times and organisms in which the experience occurs. It is purely the universal immediacy of experience that is making any such places, times or organisms 'this one'.

Be in no doubt about the radical character of what I am saying. If this experience you are having is occurring more than once, in different places, in different times—in any place, any time in all reality—then this very experience, with you within it, felt as this one, here and now, exists fully and equally in each and every one of those places and times.

When I experience myself as a philosopher talking about 'me' and 'here' and 'now', I would be badly mistaken to gesture outwards to 'others' in precise duplications of 'this' experience who are supposedly 'out there' in different places and times. I, the gesturer, am at once each and every one of those precisely similar gesturers, and the experience of gesturing to what is supposedly out there beyond is numerically that one and the same experience in each and every one of those places and times. All the places it is are equally here, all the times are equally now and all the havers of this experience are equally this person, me.

17. VARIATIONS OF MY LIFE WITHIN ETERNAL RECURRENCE

We have been talking about cases in which the experiential content is precisely repeated or duplicated. Unificationism collapses all the objective occurrences into a single experience of that content. But how are variations rather than duplications of content related to each other? Here is where we put unificationism aside and argue more simply for universalism.

What about variations of my life in eternal recurrence? This is a topic never considered by Nietzsche. Before the world of eternal recurrence could have struck a precise repetition of my life, it must first have gone through an immense number of variations of my life—slightly varied, greatly varied and in between. We can know that simply because there are so many more ways that my life could have been varied than that only one way that it could have been precisely repeated.

Remember how we rejected the insulating view of recurrence after we imagined ourselves present at the moment the sperm cell met the egg in the next recurrence and asked how that repeated event could have been prevented from being once again the calling forth of me into existence—as just such an event was indeed the calling forth of me when I came into existence in the present occurrence of my life. We asked whether some metaphysical watchman would have been there saying, 'Hey, wait a minute, this is a later occurrence so the person can't be the same'.

Well, as sperm cell meets egg (and need this be precisely the same in every detail?) in what will be a variation instead of a precise repetition of my life, is there a metaphysical watchman there ruling that it can't be me 'because the life is going to be a little different' or, even, 'because the life is going to be very different'? In any beginning of the life of a conscious thing, anywhere and anytime, something would be happening that is essentially like what we agreed would have restored me to living again—though in almost every case, of course, followed by experiential content that would be different from and therefore additional to what I am experiencing now. What could prevent that life from being mine? (Note that what we are really doing here is stretching Nietzsche's pretty well irresistible anti-insulating view—the view that it must still be me in a perfect recurrence—into a full-fledged universalism in which any conscious life is mine.)

Even within unificationism such variations, as opposed to precise repetitions and duplications, must be counted as additional experience for me. And this deluge of immensely varied life experiences would totally destroy the emphasis, so treasured by Nietzsche in his idea of recurrence, on developing the excellence of specifically the life you are living now.

18. VARIATIONS OF MY EXPERIENCE ACROSS REALITY INCLUDING SIMULTANEOUS MUTUALLY EXCLUDING EXPERIENTIAL CONTENTS

Unificationism says that I, along with this very experience I am having, would be numerically the same in precise duplications of the experience across all of reality. But what about variations of the content of experience, and of me? According to universalism I am in all of that and it is all of it mine because of the abstract quality of immediacy that permeates it all. All of it is experienced as this, here, now and mine purely because of its universal in-my-faceness.

What can make it hard to see this as possible are two mistakes. One is the confinement of my identity to only one of the organisms that are having experience. In our discussion of unification, we already saw that I would be there in all those distinct organisms that were having precisely similar experiential content. Well, I'm still there in all the variations.

The other mistake we naturally did not address when talking about precise duplications. That mistake is to think it impossible that I have varied experiential contents, excluding one another, at objectively the same time.

We can see clearly the sort of mistake this is if we briefly return to the magic film of my life. Recall that playing the quarters of my life in objectively differing orders resulted in no change at all in the subjective experience of my life. (Remember that any way we choose to line up our alphabet blocks has no effect on the alphabetical order of the letters.)

It will be useful, then, to notice that playing all the quarters of my life simultaneously also could not change my subjective experience of that life—as one quarter following another—despite the prejudice that confuses subjective with objective time.

This prejudice is part of what makes it hard to understand brain bisection, in which the same one person experiences two mutually excluding experiential contents simultaneously, as well as universalism, in which I am all conscious beings having mutually excluding experiential contents that may be objectively simultaneous.

(I leave out that the notion of 'objective simultaneity' is anyway rejected by physics.)

19. THE SPLIT-BRAIN ILLUSION

Brain bisection, the surgical cutting of the connection between the hemispheres of the brain at the bridge of nerves that normally joins them (the corpus callosum), was an operation that gave relief to epileptics. But experimenters working with split-brain patients in the 1960s discovered an additional result of this surgery that was startling and disturbing. When they fed markedly different information into each hemisphere, the subject would, it seemed, possess two mutually excluding experiences at one time.

In a somewhat simplified example, if a subject whose hands are out of sight, under a table, is given a spoon to hold in one hand and a brush in the other and afterwards asked to point to a picture of what was being held, the subject would with each hand only be able to point to the picture of the object that that hand had held. As we might say, one hand wouldn't have known what the other was doing.

Let us engage in a variation on a thought experiment in Derek Parfit's paper 'Personal Identity' that dramatises the puzzle in brain bisection. Imagine that by pressing a button I could cause a device to anaesthetise my corpus callosum, so that the communication between the hemispheres of my brain could be stopped temporarily.

I desperately want to devote this evening to listening to a certain concert—an evening-long broadcast of my favourite music, but I also have to spend all evening doing some tedious studying based on a recording of a long boring lesson. Well, why don't I arrange that the music will go into only the right hemisphere (which is musical) while the study material will go into only the left (which is verbal) after the button has been pushed to stop the integration of the activities of the hemispheres and thus any distraction of either by the other? But now a big question arises: What will my evening be like?

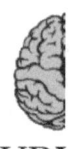 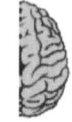

STUDYING   CONCERT
(NO CONCERT)   (NO STUDYING)

Think about this: *Someone* just slogs through the studying. And *someone* just enjoys the concert. But is it me in both cases? Or am I doing one while someone new does the other? Or have a couple of new someones taken my place?

Note that the continuing identities of the hemispheres and of the branching thought processes are not at all problematic like the question of which of these are then mine. The hemispheres could be easily distinguished and their distinct histories charted over time, as could the branching development of the thought into that about the concert and that about the studying. The problem, then, cannot be in the identification of these hemispheres or branchings. The problem is rather what would be making one of them or neither of them or both of them mine instead of somebody else's.

The usual understanding of what a person is does not allow that I could be both enjoying the concert and suffering through the studying, since each of these experiences seems walled off from the person who is having the other. Yet it cannot be that I only enjoy the concert or alternatively only suffer through the studying or that I somehow experience neither.

For, following a more extensive anaesthetising, or a stroke, that completely incapacitated one hemisphere, I would certainly have had whichever experience was in the remaining functioning hemisphere. The concert experience would be mine if there were only the right hemisphere and the studying would be mine if there were only the left. In our case there are both. How could either experience fail to be mine merely because another one is taking place across the way?

Furthermore, after the anaesthetic wears off and the integration of activities in the hemispheres has returned, I will remember having had both experiences equally well. I will remember both as having been mine. But it cannot be that the memory is somehow retroactively making both to have been mine It is rather that I am discovering what had been true at the time but had then been hidden because of the lack of integration—that both experiences were mine when I had them.

Notice that the split-brain case is raising the question about the experience of time that I discussed in the previous section. There seems to be a problem because of the objective simultaneity of the mutually excluding contents of experience. How could one person have two such mutually excluding contents of experience *at the same time*?

Well, a barn can be both red and not red at the same time—in different places on its surface. If all experience at any time is actually mine (and all the possessors of it are therein me), then there is plenty of room for such simultaneous variations. So, there is obviously no problem of logic with this simultaneous possession of mutually excluding experience.

Neither is there a phenomenological problem. As I've already pointed out, when the block is removed and the integration of the hemispheres resumes, I will be able to remember having had experience both of the concert and the studying. These past contents of my experience will then be looked upon by me as in the same sort of relation to each other, and to me, as any two mutually excluding contents of experience that had instead in the usual way not occurred in the same objective time.

But what if in the original procedure the concert experience had been run through first while the other hemisphere was kept inactive and then the studying had been run through while the concert hemisphere had been kept inactive? Thus, each experience would have occurred at an objectively different time. So what? They'd be remembered in just the same way, as simply two experiences that were mine. Yet only like this could they have satisfied the mistaken requirement of not running simultaneously. How could this really be making any difference to whose experience these were? Our earlier discussion has established that the objective times at which experience occurs are irrelevant not only to the feeling of the experience but to its identity. All experience feels like—and therein is—mine and now no matter where and when it occurs.

The answer to what my evening will be like, then, must be that I will experience both the concert and the studying, *though each will seem falsely to be the whole of my experience at that time*. It is this same false seeming that hides the fact that *all* experience actually is mine, now and at all times—and therefore yours. All the experience in all the separate nervous systems of the world is mine, *though what is discovered in each necessarily seems falsely to be the whole of what is mine*.

For what makes an experience mine is none of the specification of its content or of the particularity or other properties of experiencing organisms.

All that is required for an experience to be mine is that it be immediate in its character—that it be first-person. That was all that made both the studying and the listening to the concert my experience. When they were later remembered as mine, what was crucial was only that both were remembered as having been immediate, in the first-person style.

20. BRAIN BISECTION AND SELF-INTEREST

Imagine that you are fitted with a button like that described above that can temporarily disconnect the hemispheres of your brain. Suppose you are preparing for an evening in which your left hemisphere will be employed in dreary studying while your right hemisphere is taking in an enjoyable concert—each experience isolated from the other.

Now imagine that, with a bit of effort beforehand, you could eliminate an annoying hum from the audio equipment you'll be using for both the study and the concert. That improvement would enhance both experiences. What kind of motivation would justify taking the trouble?

If you thought of yourself as improving the experience of others—of conscious beings who, after the hemispheric split, would not be you—then the appropriate motivation might be sympathy. But if those later experiences are each yours in your thinking, then it would be illogical for your motivation to be sympathy. You would not be acting for the sake of someone else. You would be acting in self-interest.

According to the reasoning in the previous section, self-interest rather than sympathy is the appropriate motivation. Both the studying and the concert will be your experiences. You will be the one having each, though each will falsely seem to be the whole of your experience at that time. The bisection only creates a misleading appearance of separateness—not an actual separation of selves.

And so it is, according to universalism, in all cases. When you act in relation to the experiences of any conscious being, it is self-interest—not sympathy (and certainly not apathy or antipathy)—that is appropriate. All that disconnected experience is equally yours. Only you are the one inside it, having it.

But this does not mean that you should simply trample on all the motivations that are powerfully inspired by the illusion of separate self-interests. An unthinking fanaticism would make you miserable over and over. Try to be intelligent and sensitive in applying this knowledge to your treatment of yourself.

21. DEATH, WHERE IS YOUR STING?

Some of what we have seen regarding the distinction between objective and subjective time should help us understand what happens beyond death.

Subjective experience generally contains strong impressions of the order in the objective events that generate it. So, we may naturally look for what happens next subjectively after the objective ceasing of experience in an organism as though this must, despite that ceasing, be an experience connected to or flowing from what has then happened to that organism. In fact, there is after the cessation of experience in an organism no single next subjective moment following on in the way that the single series of previous experiences might have led us to expect. (Of course, in standard views of an afterlife, which I'm ignoring here, there would be such a straightforward continuation of the thing that you are or have become at death and your subjective stream would simply continue with it.)

What comes next subjectively after the very last conscious moment of an organism's life cannot be experience paradoxically turning into eternal non-experience. Larkin's imagery in his poem 'Aubade' of being 'lost in' 'the sure extinction' may suggest this mistake, but for the most part in the poem he is dreading the cessation of experience altogether (as in 'Not here, not anywhere')—which is all too appropriate a fear within the usual view of confined personal identity.

But my identity is not bound by the objective limits of any organism. I am whatever has experience, and I cannot somehow become something that exists apart from experience—like a permanently insensible corpse or like non-experiencing nothing. So, what is death like for the genuine me?

Every moment of experience is, within it, subjectively that experience happening now, which gives every moment the subjective status also of the experience that has just come about as next (whether or not the experience relates itself, through memories, to some past of experiences).

So, subjectively I won't be without a next experience. All experience is equally next experience subjectively. And I cannot fail to be in any of it. Though, of course it won't all be experienced as though it's somehow happening at the same time. Each is cut off from the other next experiences. Each subjective moment will more or less position itself as occurring in a stream of objective events that shaped it.

It seems to me all right to think of death as equivalent subjectively to an objective process of reincarnation—or rather, countless such processes—wherein an experience subjectively next is each and every experience. I am simply there in all of it, and I am nowhere apart from possessing the capacity for experience.

We know there is lots of consciousness—and all of it has to be mine. But what if it had been the case that there was little or no consciousness in all reality? Well, if there had been no consciousness I would never have existed.

In the case of there having been only little consciousness, I would of course have been the experiencer in it. Note that this could not have been a subjectively prolonged experience if it was not an experience of prolongation of experience. So, it would not have been experienced as eternal, even though it would have been experienced purely as now and even though its objective nonexistence before or after it would have to have been nothing subjective for me. Such a stingy reality would have provided me with nothing more beyond death. But the actual reality I am in does provide me with an enormous quantity of varied experience—and all of it necessarily mine.

Reality with little experience would be like my experience being confined by the false boundary around the just one me in the usual view. My thought of what it would be like for me in that reality with little experience therefore arouses in me a claustrophobic feeling like Larkin's in 'Aubade'. But the actual vastness of the experience that is mine beyond the false boundaries of me makes nonsense of this feeling.

If reality is large enough, it contains variations of the life you now know. You and the people you know would be there as you and those people (really also you)—not mere copies who are internally others, but the very same—because of the truth of universalism.

22. NAGEL'S PROBLEM

In a famous thought experiment,[1] the philosopher Thomas Nagel asks us to consider an ideally comprehensive description of everything in the world that is entirely neutral in the sense that it is not anchored exclusively to the perspective of just one particular person, place or time (although it does include within it a full description of the perspectives of every person, place and time). He imposed this neutrality of perspective on the ideally comprehensive description in what may appear a somewhat technical fashion regarding language—by stipulating that this description contained no 'token-reflexive expressions'.

Token-reflexive expressions are used to refer to things from a particular perspective to which the expressions themselves are anchored by the individual occurrences—the tokens—of the words. Examples are 'I', 'me', 'you', 'here', 'there', 'now', 'then', 'yesterday' and 'tomorrow'.

---

1.   Thomas Nagel, 'Physicalism', *The Philosophical Review* 74 (1965): the quotations that follow are from pages 354–355.

So, the description of the world Nagel has in mind is one that does not originate from any one perspective. There's no particular 'I' or 'now' that it is centred on. It is also a description that is aimed at comprehending everything ('everything that can be said about the world without employing any token-reflexive expressions').

And therefore, though originating from no particular perspective, the description would by no means be lacking in perspective*s* (plural) in its content. For a description that aspired to a perfect comprehensiveness would need to include within it a description of all the perspectives that sentient beings will occupy. (Notice that it would not necessarily endorse the perceptions had and the judgments made from those perspectives but it would have to register perfectly what all of these were like.)

And so (after mentioning the exhaustive account of all straightforwardly physical things and their states in the ideal description we are considering) Nagel says, 'It will also include a description of all the persons in the world and their histories, memories, thoughts, sensations, perceptions, intentions and so forth. I can thus describe without token-reflexives the entire world and everything that is happening in it—and this will include a description of Thomas Nagel and what he is thinking and feeling'.

Let me point out that there will, then, have to be many token-reflexive expressions showing up in this description after all; but all of these will be, at least figuratively, placed within quotes, as used in the description of what it is like to be within each and every perspective that the world contains. These perspectives are all contained neutrally. The description does not identify itself with any one of them. There will be no unquoted I, here and now belonging to a describer of the world who occupies some single particular perspective within the world. But the description does fully record all the specialness that such perspectives will naturally be ascribing to themselves.

Then Nagel goes on, 'Even when everything that can be said in the specified manner has been said, and the world has in a sense been completely described, there seems to remain one fact which has not been expressed, and that is the fact that I am Thomas Nagel. This is not, of course, the fact ordinarily conveyed by those words, when they are used to inform someone else who the *speaker* is—for that could easily be expressed otherwise. It is rather the fact that *I* am the subject of *these* experiences; this body is my body; the subject or centre of my world is this person, Thomas Nagel'. (It would also seem that other, similar facts had remained unexpressed—like that this place is here, this time is now and a particular day is tomorrow.)

I have already pointed out that there must be in such a description the fullest recognition of the perspectival character of the experience of conscious beings, as might be represented in the use of something like quoted token-reflexives. And Nagel himself points out that his own thoughts are included.

So, let me simply pinpoint that any complete such description would have to register (though in quoted fashion, of course) the very thought that Nagel is having when he says that '*I* am the subject of *these* experiences'. Well, then, is he not therein expressing the fact he has in mind, and thus expressing it within the description? So how can there yet seem to be a fact expressed in Nagel's thought but not expressed in the description?

What makes this inclusion of Nagel's thought in the description fail to be a proper expression of what Nagel means to be thinking is that, as it occurs within that description, Nagel's thinking that thought can be clearly seen to be nothing special, nothing capable of distinguishing him from any others. For the comprehensive description reveals that every conscious state would equally feel itself to be the only one that was 'this consciousness, this experience'.

And that seeming exclusivity, as the one and only experience that was 'this experience', would within each experience seem to be a most impressive and important fact. After all, the subject would seem to be discovering its own identity, as the sole fit subject of its own self-interest, by picking itself out as 'this subject', 'me', from within the only experience that was 'this experience'. '*I* am the subject of *these* experiences', as Nagel says. And it is having experiences that are *these* as opposed to *those* (other experiences) that gives self-interest and urgency all its bite. The only pain that really hurts me is *this* special one, the one experienced here and now as mine.

An experience being this as opposed to that (other experience) could have nothing to do with any of the specifications of either its subjective content or its objective context. After all, with the very same specifications in its content and its context it will count as this experience from within it and as that (other experience) from outside it.

This experience is just what any experience is within itself, from the inside. The internal immediacy is all that makes any experience be for itself *this* one, *now* (in other words, at *this* time), *here* (at *this* place) and *mine* (belonging to *this* experiencer). And all experiences have being *this* one equally within them. All are *this, now, here* and *mine*. It's just the immediacy.

Earlier I talked about what made my experience be mine. The same points apply at once to any experience being this, here, and now as well as mine. It is not due at all to any of the detail of the content of the experience. If the colours I was seeing had been different, my experience would not have failed to be this and mine. If I had fallen asleep and was now in the middle of a wild dream that had little in common with any of the usual content of my experience, that would not have somehow therein failed to be experienced as this and mine. If I had eaten different particular items of food over the past years (as I might so easily have done), so that all the particular atoms in the structure of my body were different in numerical identity from those in my body now, the experience would not on that account have failed to have that character of being this and mine. In a different objective place and time, it would still have been this, here, now and mine.

What makes an experience this, here, now and mine is none of the specification of its content or of the particularity or other properties of its possessor, place or time. All that is required for an experience to be this one is that it be immediate in its character.

There seems to be a fact that must elude what also seems to be an ideally comprehensive description, but this 'fact' is just an illusion of perspective.

23. THE WRITER AND THE READER

Let's look at the case of the two of us, the writer of this discussion and the reader of it: Could we discover as expressed in a description of both of us that was made without the use of unquoted token-reflexives that one of these, writer or reader, was you and the other was me?

Well, can't I just find myself, the writer, the one who is called 'Arnold Zuboff', in the description? Yes, I can find someone called 'Arnold Zuboff' there, but what in the description we are considering expresses that he's me and not you rather than the other way around?

Well, he would be the possessor of this experience, of writing, and could therefore from within the experience identify the one called 'Zuboff' as this experiencer, 'me'. But, of course, in the description we see clearly that each experience, of writing or of reading, is equally discovered to be exclusively 'this experience' from within it and that each experiencer is equally discovered to be exclusively 'this experiencer', 'me'.

But if, as I am tempted to think, the person I am just *is* the one called 'Arnold Zuboff', isn't the distinction that exists in the description between Arnold Zuboff and the reader enough in itself to distinguish the person who is me from the other who is you? It is tempting to think, then, that I am properly discovered to be me when the Zuboff in that description is picking himself out as 'me'. (This is, of course, just like the occurrence of Nagel's thought within the description of the world made without unquoted token-reflexives.)

But no, drawing this objective distinction between organisms must still be useless at expressing on which side of the distinction I fall till it has been somehow expressed in the description that I am indeed the one called 'Arnold Zuboff' and not the reader. They both pick themselves out as 'me'. There is nothing expressed in the description that could possibly distinguish which was you from which was me. Each in that description would be seen to be me, with the other you, as far as it was concerned.

Just as Nagel claimed, then, there does at any rate 'seem' to be a missing fact—that one of them is really me while the other is (if you'll forgive me for putting it this way) merely you.

But where do I discover this alleged fact? Perhaps I can discover it from *outside* the description, from this, my 'own' perspective (as I take it to be)? But all my efforts to distinguish myself either inside *or outside* the description must be futile. For it is illusory to think that my 'own' perspective can occupy some special privileged position lying outside the description. Every perspective is there within the description. The description is merely revealing the truth about every perspective, that there is nothing distinctive about its being 'mine'.

As Nagel claimed, there *seems* to be a missing fact—that only one is me, that one of these is really me, while the other is merely you.

But a description of everything in the world that can be described without the employment of unquoted token-reflexives plainly must show us the whole of the world as it actually is (if we may put aside any unconnected problems with whether everything of the world is describable). There could be nothing that is real outside it.

It seems to me that any perfectly comprehensive description must conform to the prohibition imposed by Nagel because any perfectly comprehensive description could not be confined to any one perspective. A description that was confined to a perspective would be by definition partial—and would be open to illusion. Could we, then, have lost anything that was real just because our description of reality was the properly comprehensive one?

Let's briefly throw into our consideration the parallel question regarding a time being this time, being now. From within the experience of my writing of this discussion the time of the writing is now and the time of your reading is then, sometime in the future. From within the experience of your reading the writing would be then, in the past, while the reading would be this time, now. So, is there an additional fact that the time of the writing or of the reading is the one that is really now?

What I think about both questions, concerning both the time and the experiencer, could be stated in two claims:

1. Being me is settled simply by the first-person perspective of an organism's experience rather than by the identity of the organism itself. One can

find nothing in the identity of an organism to make it me apart from this perspective it has on itself, as being 'this subject'. With that it is me; without that it is not me. Being now is settled by the present-tense character of the experience rather than the objective identity of the time in which the experience is occurring. In both cases there is a similar illusion—that being me is based on the objective identity conditions of the organism happening to be the ones required for it to be me or that my experience being now is based on the time of the experience happening to be a unique objective present.

2. There is a mere illusion of uniqueness in each such perspective. Being me seems like the only being me and being now seems like the only being now. That is why they fasten themselves onto the objective conditions of the experience. For these *do* have uniqueness. The reality is that all conscious organisms are equally experienced as 'me' and all experienced times are equally experienced as 'now'. And that's all there is to the determinations of being me and now. They are subjective despite seeming objective.

Notice that I certainly am not saying there is *no* real me. On the contrary, I am saying that being me—really being me—extends equally to all conscious things.

And so what I am saying has spectacular implications: It means that my self-interest reaches fully into the life of every conscious organism, each of which I equally am, and that the death of any one of these does not annihilate me so long as there still is any other conscious thing anywhere in all reality—since I will be that thing. And every experience in any time is experienced by me with all the same urgency of its happening now. All of it equally is mine and now.

It follows that inflicting pain as retribution for wrongs is a horrible mistake: The person who was wronged and the person who is punished are one and the same.

Let me stress that I don't ever wish to be questioning the distinctness from each other of different times or the distinctness from each other of different organisms. I'm assuredly not saying there's only one time or only one organism.

What I am challenging is that it is a fact that some one of those distinct times is the only one that is now and that it is a fact that some one of those distinct organisms is the only one that is me. And if none of those organisms is exclusively me, if the seeming to be so in each of them is just an illusion of perspective, then it is wrong to consider those distinct organisms to be also distinct as experiencers, as persons, as mes (plural of 'me').

They would all turn out—distinct as they are as organisms—to be the same experiencer, the same person, the same me. As me, they would be the same. (Though just how this is put is unimportant if the understanding is there. We might express this as 'all persons are me' or rather as 'you and I are the same person'. We are interested here in the things and not the language.)

When I see the truth of this, should I change in my daily life how I speak about all these conscious beings that I am? Well, that would depend on how valuable in the circumstances it would be to do so.

Think of watching a play in which the same one actor takes all the parts. It could often make sense to use the differing character names in describing what was happening on the stage. Yet it could become important on occasion as well to use the actor's single name to highlight that one person is playing all.

Words like 'this', 'now' and 'I' can continue being enormously useful in picking out particular mental contents, particular objects, particular times and organisms. They can as ever refer to things that have the right connections to the mouths that speak them, the hands that write them and the thoughts in which they occur.

24. CONCLUSION OF PART I

You possess all conscious life. Whenever in all time and wherever in all the universe (or beyond) any conscious being stands, sits, crawls, jumps, lies, rolls, flies or swims, its experience of doing so is yours and is yours now. You *are* that being. You are fish and fowl. Deer and hunter. You are saints and sinners. You are Germans, Jews and Palestinians.

This is an important result. What else can come close to it in importance? And perhaps the spread of this knowledge among the intelligent beings that are you can help you to stop yourself from hurting yourself because you mistake yourself for another.

Part II:
The A Priori Foundation of Empirical Reasoning

I lay out the logic of empirical discovery.

Next, I'll be laying the groundwork for an argument in which you will turn your own existence into evidence that will establish decisively for you that the usual view of personal identity must be rejected as absurdly improbable and replaced by universalism. Then an extension of that argument will open to us the great secret of the nature of the physical world. But a thorough understanding of the argument and its extension requires a general understanding of how we discover anything.

I strove to develop that general understanding of empirical reasoning in a talk whose written version you see below.

The talk started with a typical skeptic's challenge to the audience regarding whether they were justified in believing that they were attending the talk.

HOW TO SOLVE THE PROBLEM OF INDUCTION AND ANSWER SCEPTICISM (A TALK)

1. Are You Really at a Talk?

You can't doubt that it now *seems* to you that you are at a talk, but this immediately known mental content, the seeming, would not be contradicted by any number of skeptical hypotheses regarding the world beyond it—you are dreaming or your brain is being fed this pattern of stimulation in a vat or a malicious demon is deceiving you or there is simply no external world at all.

2. Classic Scepticism

Classic scepticism accepts the present mental content (such as that it now seems to you that you are at a talk) as properly known by you incorrigibly and accepts also knowledge of a priori necessary truth, like that 2+3=5, whose denial would be a contradiction. But the logical distinctness between

Finding Myself: Beyond the False Boundaries of Personal Identity
Special Supplement, *Midwest Studies in Philosophy*
https://doi.org/10.5840/msp202549Supplement5

current mental content and whatever else may exist is claimed to make impossible any intellectual justification, by way of necessary truth, of your usual beliefs about the external world.

3. The Problem of Induction

The problem of induction is very similar but somewhat less radical, in that it is raised within a stipulation that you have had a real past of observations. We shall start with solving this problem and then apply our solution to the more radical classic scepticism.

4. A Question About Humebirds

We arrive on a newly discovered island. So far we have observed at random times and places on the island (and tagged as observed) a hundred examples of the new species we call 'humebirds'; and all have been blue. And we have come to believe that the next humebird we see will also be blue. But how is it that we form this belief?

5. Logical Distinctness

David Hume, the most famous raiser of this problem, allows us the stipulated observations and allows us also knowledge of a priori necessary truth, like that 2+3=5, whose denial would be a contradiction. But there is a logical distinctness between the past observations and the expected next observation and between the other humebird characteristics and the colour blue. There can be no contradiction, therefore, in the next humebird being other than blue; and, it seems, we therefore have no intellectual justification for believing it will be blue by way of any necessary truth.

6. A Mere Habit of Expectation

This inspires Hume to claim that it is only a non-intellectual instinct that forms such beliefs—as a mere habit of expectation that builds in us with the repetition of observations of this same merely contingently related combination of characteristics.

7. What Hume Failed to Notice

What Hume failed to notice was the implicit reasoning that we are engaged in when we form such inductive beliefs. What we do is apply to our observations a certain necessary truth about mathematical probability—we engage in an implicit reasoning that gives us our intellectually justified confidence in a conclusion like the next humebird being blue.

8. Reasoning About Humebirds

Here is our reasoning: As we observe more and more humebirds, we are implicitly forming a belief about the general population we are sampling. With each new observation of nothing but blue humebirds it is becoming less and less probable that we would not have come across a non-blue humebird unless the humebird population was generally blue. And it is that reasoning that makes us rightly believe in a growing probability that the next humebird we observe will be blue. In other words, our observations so far of purely blue humebirds would have been an improbable event if the humebird population was not generally blue; and it is improbable that what happened in our observing was something improbable.

It is always most probable that the most probable thing will occur—or has occurred. This remains true in cases where it is most probable, given all the evidence, that an improbable event has occurred because other things would have to be interpreted as even more improbable than the improbable event in question if that event had not occurred. I call this a 'strained' improbability. It remains a suspect undigested improbability for those who are forced to accept it by the threat of that greater improbability if it is rejected.

The necessary principle that the most probable is most probable and the improbable is improbable is also not breached in cases of what I call 'relaxed' improbability, where the observation of a locally strained improbable event is made to be probable as viewed within a non-local perspective that is wide enough to include many chances for such an event to occur. We'll look more at the perspectival character of probability later.

It has occurred to me that the understanding I have developed of empirical reasoning might be called 'proto-Bayesian', since it proceeds not from Bayes' theorem, but from the deep necessary principle I have stated that underlies it.

9. Going Deeper

Let's go deeper regarding the humebirds. Our inference must reach beyond the mere generality of the blueness to the causes of that. If, for example, the hidden genetic workings of humebird colour had meant it was merely an improbable fluke that the humebirds were generally blue, yet they were, then that hypothesis of generally blue humebirds—but merely by fluke—could not have succeeded in making our observations probable. The general blueness has to be determined and stable.

10. The Urns Case

Let me describe another case of such reasoning. Imagine there are two urns, one containing a million tiny blue beads and the other also containing a million tiny beads but only one of them blue. One of these urns is pushed forward. We reach in without looking, stir them thoroughly, and pull out just one bead. If it is a blue bead, we infer that the urn pushed forward was overwhelmingly more probable to have been the one with all blue beads. How?

11. Reasoning About Beads

The blue bead is our evidence, and according to our stipulations there are just two hypotheses available to explain that evidence. The hypothesis that the urn pushed forward was the urn that contained only one blue bead is not at all impossible. There's no contradiction between the evidence and the truth of that hypothesis. Yet there is indeed a contradiction between that hypothesis obtaining and the evidence being probable. For within that hypothesis itself it is required that our evidence would have been an extremely improbable event. But, it is improbable that what happened when we drew out that blue bead was something improbable.

12. The Overall Hypothesis

In this case too, as with the humebirds, we can go deeper. What determined which urn was pushed forward? We haven't been told. But we can infer that the probabilities that governed the pushing forward of the urns, the 'prior probabilities' of the two hypotheses, probably did not favour the pushing forward of the urn containing only one blue bead. For that 'overall hypothesis', as we might call it, would have required one of two improbable things to have happened. Either the all blue urn was pushed forward, which is supposed to be improbable, or else the urn with one blue bead was pushed forward, which would have made the drawing of the blue bead improbable. The overall hypothesis with no improbability is that the prior probabilities favoured the urn that itself favoured the evidence. And thus, that's what we must infer to be most probably true.

13. A Great Imbalance

Inferences in cases where competing hypotheses are close to each other in how probable they would make the occurrence of the evidence can be very sensitive to prior probabilities. If one urn contained a hundred percent blue beads and the other ninety-nine percent, and a blue bead was drawn out, then knowing the prior probabilities governing the pushing forward of the urns would figure very large in judging the probability of which urn was pushed forward. But nearly all the cases that shall concern us will involve instead a very great imbalance between the hypotheses regarding the probability of the evidence. And in all such cases the prior probabilities can safely be inferred, as we have seen, to have favoured hypotheses that themselves favour the evidence.

14. Rejecting the Ad Hoc as Improbable

We must reject as improbable any merely ad hoc specifications in hypotheses, designed ad hoc ('to this' in Latin) to force the evidence to emerge from an otherwise unfavourable hypothesis. A hypothesis in which there were only a hundred humebirds that were blue but it is ad hoc specified that by chance they were the only ones so far observed doesn't make those observations any more probable to have occurred since the specification itself is improbable within the hypothesis itself given the general character of the hypothesis. The same of course goes for specifying in the hypothesis of the urn containing only one blue bead in a million that it was an urn in which the blue bead was drawn out by chance. That specification would indeed seem to guarantee its being drawn out but its being drawn out would not have become a jot more probable within the hypothesis.

15. Reasoning, Not Habit

Let me now use the example of the urns to drive home the point that we are not forming habits of expectation, as Hume thought we were, in arriving at inductive beliefs. It is obvious that we cannot have been doing that when we drew out only one blue bead and concluded that the urn being sampled was that with all blue beads. This was reasoning about probability and involved no repetition at all.

But now imagine that there is only one urn about which we are told nothing. Without peeking into it we reach in and feel many beads. And we begin drawing them out one by one, reaching all around within the urn to make sure that we are randomly sampling the whole of it. Now we have pulled out a hundred beads, all of them blue. We have formed a belief that the next will be blue. How? We are implicitly reasoning that it would be improbable to have drawn out beads that were all blue unless the bead population in the urn was generally blue. Here we do have repetition. But we are not, or not merely, forming a non-intellectual habit of expectation regarding these beads. And we could alter the case so that we moved our hand around gathering those beads from random places in the urn and drew them all out at once. Our belief would be precisely the same and there would have been no forming of a habit through repetition.

16. A Loaded Coin and the Sun

Let me add another example. A coin has been tossed a thousand times and every time landed heads. There are only two coins available, one fair and the other loaded to land heads. We believe that the next time it is tossed the coin will land heads, not because we have formed a habit of expectation but because within the fair coin hypothesis this evidence, though possible, would have to have been an extremely improbable occurrence—and it is necessarily improbable that something improbable is what has occurred.

This coin example is very much like Hume's own famous case of the sun's rising every morning. We expect that to continue not because of a habit of expectation but because its having done so with such great consistency is evidence for the hypothesis that, like a loaded coin, there is something that reliably makes it do so. A hypothesis in which its rising stopped tomorrow would either need to represent its previous risings as also precarious and therefore improbable or need to posit a cut off point for its past stability that was merely ad hoc specified as not having occurred before tomorrow and yet occurring tomorrow.

17. The Probabilities Not Discovered Empirically

Notice, by the way, that the probabilities involved in such reasoning are all fixed a priori within the hypotheses and are not somehow circularly learned through induction. We don't learn empirically that it would be improbable for a fair coin to land heads a thousand times consecutively. That is a necessary truth about a fair coin. The observations, of course, are acquired empirically; but the probabilities that might apply to them if we interpret them as being one thing or another are decided a priori in the hypotheses.

(Let me take a moment using the case of the thousand heads to say something about prediction vs purely past observation as the basis of such reasoning. There is a view that predictions are superior, or even required, for arriving at empirical conclusions. Well, imagine that after the five hundredth coin flip during the thousand someone had made a prediction that the coin would continue to land heads—a prediction that had then proved true. Does whether or not someone had happened to utter such words at the midpoint in the thousand coin flips make a bit of difference to the legitimacy or force of the inference based on the thousand straight heads? I don't think so.)

18. Probability Is Perspectival

There's much more we can say about the probability reasoning that underlies and justifies induction. For example, all probability is perspectival. From the perspective of the winner of a lottery the event is an improbable lucky coincidence whereas from the perspective of a non-involved observer of the lottery it is just someone winning and therefore not improbable at all. And this perspectival character of the improbability itself naturally carries over to inferences that are based on judging hypotheses to be improbable.

19. The Humebird Inference Is Perspectival

Imagine countless earth-like planets viewed by God on each of which creatures like humebirds with only a hundred blue in their populations and the rest non-blue are being randomly observed by discoverers of islands. It would not be improbable for God if in a very small fraction of these countless events the first hundred observed were all blue by chance. But it would still rightly be judged improbable by the local observers, and that would mislead them into inferring that the next such bird would be blue. They would be wrong in their expectation but right in their basis for it. Even when these misled observers eventually discover the truth about the whole bird population, so that they have all the information God does about it, they will rightly count their situation as improbable for them though it won't be improbable for God.

20. Isn't All of It Improbable Anyway?

Recognising the perspectival character of probability and inference allows us to escape the widespread confusion according to which every time a card is drawn from a deck or a roulette wheel is spun, the event of, say, the deuce of spades being removed or the ball landing at 26 possesses only a single low probability.

The event of randomly picking a deuce of spades from a deck has a multiplicity of descriptions that could be assigned truly to it, with some of these descriptions carrying conflicting probabilities. It is 'drawing the deuce of spades' (1 in 52), 'drawing a deuce' (1 in 13), 'drawing a spade' (1 in 4), 'not drawing the queen of hearts' (51 in 52), 'drawing some card or other' (52 in 52). So how could it be merely an event having a probability of 1 in 52?

If a meteorite lands in the Forest of Dean, that one event has a number of differing probabilities—from very high to very low. There's the great probability of the earth being hit, the lower probability of the northern hemisphere being hit, still lower probability of England being hit, the yet lower probability of the Forest of Dean being hit, the still lower probability of that sector of the forest being hit and the extremely low probability of that very spot being hit.

The improbabilities only come into play when a coincidence highlighting one of these areas occurs within a perspective independently linked to that area. If I am walking in the forest when the meteorite strikes, that is an improbable coincidence for me—whose precise improbability would depend on how close to me it hits. But for someone in Australia with an interest in meteorites who merely learns of the strike there is no improbable coincidence and no improbability.

A meteorite actually hitting a human would be an improbable standout event for everyone on earth. Like someone winning a lottery that rarely has winners, or a lottery failing to produce any winner when it almost always does. Yet even these seemingly perspectiveless improbabilities could become probable within a perspective spanning enough time or space (as in our earlier God and the humebirds example).

A random drawing of a deuce of spades or a ball landing at 26 would only be improbable from a perspective within which that card or number had been coincidentally designated, perhaps in a guess or a bet, or in any other way. For all others it would be merely some card or other being drawn or some number or other coming up, which would involve no improbability.

When we say the probability of drawing a deuce of spades is 1 in 52 or the probability of winning a certain lottery is one in a million, what we are doing implicitly is thinking of the card or an entrant as designated independently of being selected and then rightly thinking that a match of just that card or entrant with the one that is randomly selected by the draw or the lottery would have that degree of improbability. In the case of the lottery, we can easily think imaginatively of the winning from the winner's angle, from which there is indeed an improbable match. Those thoughts thus spelled out make perfect sense. But, as often happens, if we then try to think clearly about our own thinking we can easily get confused. We may easily just think that the improbability from the angle of a match belongs to that matched event itself even without the match.

21. Isn't None of It Improbable Anyway?

Another confusion concerns determinism. The thought is that if strict determinism is true then every event must simply be certain to happen.

But if strict determinism is true, it occurs always at a very micro level of the descriptions of events. Nearly all the cases of probability that would interest us are at a very macro level, and the details of what is happening at the micro level, regardless of whether these are strictly deterministic, don't figure into their macro level probabilities. If one considers all the micro level descriptions that the trajectory of a flipped fair coin could have, only a tiny fraction of these would involve the macro level description of its landing heads a thousand times consecutively. Hence it would be improbable to the tune of one in two to the thousandth power that any randomly observed run of a thousand fair coin flips would have that macro description.

22. Solving Nelson Goodman's New Riddle of Induction

In presenting his new riddle of induction, in his book *Fact, Fiction and Forecast*, Nelson Goodman famously uses the example of discovering emeralds to be green, but I'll state his point using the discovery of humebirds to be blue.

As before, we observe the first hundred sampled humebirds to be blue. But, Goodman would say, there seems no reason that we cannot—instead of, as he puts it, 'generalizing the predicate "blue"' to the unseen rest of the humebirds—'generalize' the predicate 'bleen', which means 'blue if observed within the first hundred observations but green after that'. ('Bleen' wouldn't mean that at that stage all the birds change colour from blue to green but rather that the so-far unseen birds were always and will remain green and the observed ones were always and will remain blue.)

What Goodman does not consider in the least is that the predicate 'bleen' could only be appropriate if something extremely improbable had happened—if there were only one hundred blue humebirds and the rest green but we had happened just by chance to see only the hundred blue birds in all our first observations with none of the green ones getting mixed in. All the humebirds' being generally blue—and certainly not their being bleen—is what makes our observations a probable occurrence.

23. Turning Now to Scepticism

But let me now move on to defeating classic scepticism with the same reasoning that has solved the problem of induction.

24. The Seeming of Seeming

Rather than merely stipulating observations and then challenging where we can go from there just using necessary truth, classic scepticism gets down to what I shall claim is the proper foundation of our knowledge—merely present mental content plus necessary truth.

It seems to you that you are at a talk, with lots of seeming sensing and other mental activity. How do you know that this is how it seems to you?

Many philosophers would claim that you know this incorrigibly. Descartes says that regarding this there is 'no room for error'. If I claim to be seeing an audience, for that claim to be true there must be an audience beyond that seeming and I must be properly caused by that audience to be entertaining that state of seeming to see them. Here there is 'room for error'. But if I drop that claim down to just the existence and nature of the seeming itself that room for error is gone.

And I think we don't even have to claim certainty regarding such present mental content to use it as our evidence for inferring its causes. If somehow it merely seems to me that it seems to me that I see an audience, that would be material enough for an inference. So instead of claiming incorrigibility, I would claim contentment with the mere seeming of seeming.

25. Necessary Truth

When the mental content is a concept, we can discern in that concept what would have to be true of whatever would count as the object of that concept. In my concept of 2 added to 3, I discern that nothing could count as the object of that concept unless it was 5. The denial of 2+3=5 would be a contradiction that could therefore never exist. That is necessary truth, and it has certainty. And now let's turn to how necessary truths about probability can be applied to our present mental content in a way that gives us legitimate conclusions about what the world around us is most probably like.

26. No External World?

One particularly extreme sceptical hypothesis is that there is no world at all external to the present mental content. I, for one, cannot see that there is any logical contradiction between the existence of my present mental content and the nonexistence of anything outside it. The logical possibility of this hypothesis is owing to the logical distinctness between that mental content and anything other than it. But that doesn't mean that we can't reason regarding the mathematical probability of the character of my present mental content if there's no external world.

27. The Improbability of No External World

In my present mental content, for one thing, colours are nicely ordered into areas. If all that existed was just colour dots and other such basic constituents of a momentary awareness, their pattern would have been vastly more probable to have been chaotic. There are just so very many more chaotic ways that they could have been. There would, if there was nothing but them, be nothing that could be ordering them. It would be like the fair coin just happening to land heads a thousand times consecutively—without any loading that could cause all those heads. It would be like coloured sand randomly blown onto a tabletop presenting us with a detailed scene. Such events are necessarily improbable within such hypotheses. And crafting the hypothesis of no external world into one in which it is simply asserted that this ordered pattern happened by chance is just adding an improbable ad hoc specification to the hypothesis.

28. *The Improbability of the Malicious Demon and the Precedence of the General*

But what about other sceptical hypotheses, like the brain in the vat or Descartes' malicious demon? They, unlike the hypothesis of no external world, do provide causes that are supposed to be producing this pattern of current experience. The problem with them is that the general character of that causation, mad scientists at work on a disembodied brain or a malicious demon at work on a disembodied mind, could not make probable the sort of pattern I now have—not only of sensation but of seemingly previously formed beliefs and so on—without a purely ad hoc specification in the hypothesis that mad scientist or malicious demon bizarrely intended to produce the sort of impressions I now have of a very different and varied world containing in it many differing kinds of causes of my experience. So instead I rightly craft a hypothesis with a rich arrangement of general causes of my experience to suit the varied character of its pattern—with, for example, some causes having impersonal physical natures and others having thoughts and motivations. The world I rightly believe to be the probable cause of my experience is a world that given its general character would most probably have produced this pattern of experience.

Notice that we see here too the answer to scepticism regarding other minds.

This discussion illustrates a principle, which we could call the precedence of the general: the general character of a hypothesis governs how probable it is, not arbitrary special details merely invented to force a match with the evidence. A hypothesis whose general nature makes the evidence improbable cannot be rescued by ad hoc stipulations. Again, the malicious demon could make my impressions more probable only by positing that it bizarrely intended exactly this pattern of experience—highly improbable given the general character of such a being. Similarly, one could specify that a fair coin by chance landed heads a thousand times in a row, but this would not make the outcome genuinely probable; a loaded or double-headed coin, by contrast, does make the evidence probable by virtue of its general character. [Just so, combining your general nature in the usual view of personal identity with perfect luck in all those sperm cell lotteries is no competition for you resulting from the universal character of immediacy.]

29. Dreaming

Descartes invites us also to consider the hypothesis of dreaming. The hypothesis that I am now dreaming is certainly logically consistent with my present pattern of experience and seeming memories. But that consistency doesn't make this pattern of experience and memory any kind of evidence for the hypothesis that I am dreaming. There is nothing in my experience now that is dream-like enough to suggest dreaming as its probable cause. Rather everything suggests the styles of causes in a waking reality. This judgment is based partly, of course, on my seeming memories of and seemingly previously formed beliefs about a general contrast between the experiences of dreaming and those of the waking world. In these impressions of a past I find dreams and being awake fairly well distinguished in a way that would strongly favour the probability of my now being awake. And though my possession of such bases for distinction would be logically consistent with the hypothesis that I am merely dreaming them—and that they are false—the more probable causes of these impressions would be dreams and the world as these impressions represent them to be. My possession of all this evidence for being awake would have been improbable on the opposing hypothesis that I am dreaming, apart from ad hoc specification of the dreaming; and so the hypothesis of dreaming itself is made improbable by that evidence.

But if my seeming memories of dreams had instead represented them as having been much more like this experience, if the distinction between dream and reality were therefore harder for me to draw within this experience and its impressions of a past, then my confidence that I was not now dreaming would have been properly undermined, from within my own experience, within my evidence. And if within my experience there were powerful impressions of brain-in-the-vat scientists or malicious demons or other sorts of virtual reality enthusiasts who were somehow at large, inducing experiences much like this one in victims who were like me, I'd no longer have a right to my current confidence in the probability that my experience is a relatively unmediated product of my own knocking around in the world.

30. Simplicity, Ockham's Razor, Etc.

I think that most of the virtues that have been ascribed to good empirical thinking belong inherently to—and thus are explained by—the probability reasoning that I have been describing. For example, simplicity.

Imagine we are trying to infer the nature of an unseen curve through thinking about points on that curve that are being randomly reported to us. A simple curve will, of course, always yield points that can be interpreted as lying on a simple curve. Though any one of the numberless complex curves that could be drawn through this same set of points could indeed also have yielded them, it would be an increasingly improbable coincidence if points randomly selected from a complex curve were continuing to lie as well on some simple curve. Thus, probability requires us to favour a simple interpretation if a simple one is possible.

But, let me stress, the simplicity of the curve must be understood as resulting from some regularity in its cause. A hypothesis that would genuinely make our evidence probable must display a principled connection between the inherent character of the hypothesis and the production of that evidence. The hypothesis of a simple curve produced according to a regular principle would do this. The hypothesis of a curve that was merely simple through chance, however, would be useless for making any evidence of its simplicity probable.

The principle of sufficient reason and Ockham's razor bid us to arrive at a hypothesis containing nothing less and nothing more than what is needed to make the evidence probable. Anything more would be an unsupported probability risk.

31. How Bad Attempted Solutions Have Corrupted Philosophy, Starting with Kant

'It still remains a scandal to philosophy, and to human reason in general, that the existence of things external to us . . . must be accepted merely on faith, and that, if anyone thinks good to doubt their existence, we are unable to counter his doubts by any satisfactory proof'. (Kant, leading into his own attempted proof of the existence of the external world, in a footnote to the preface to the second edition of the *Critique of Pure Reason*.)

Recall once more our initial humebird problem. Imagine now a rather desperate attempt to establish a priori that the next humebird we observed will be blue by merely defining 'humebirds' as blue. That would indeed assure us that the next 'humebird' would have to be blue, but it would pretty obviously leave us with the substantive question unanswered, the question, as it now might be put, of whether the next bird otherwise like a humebird will be blue.

We have found, of course, that we can deal appropriately with this substantive question by establishing a priori that, given our evidence, it was necessarily probable that the next such bird would be blue. (And we can leave the definition of 'humebird' open regarding what colour one might have. After all, it is far more useful to allow nature to teach us about the natural kinds of the world than to fix them as having lots of their characteristics trivially by definition.)

Well, philosophers trying to meet the challenge of scepticism have often resembled desperate 'humebird' redefiners in that they have arrived at theories of the external world and other minds that amounted to something like defining the external world as real or other people as behaving and speaking in the way that we would normally think them to be doing. Their answers to scepticism were thus curiously trivial, restricted to mere presuppositions, of experience or of interpretation of the speech of others, or established in the rules, the criteria, for the use of our language. And these philosophers missed the proper answer to scepticism, which is the establishment of the tremendous probability of the objective reality of the external world and other minds given the evidence of the pattern of experience.

For example, Kant argued for the existence and the uniformity of an external world 'transcendentally' by claiming that our momentary present pattern of mental content deserved to be called 'experience' only if it was viewed as caused by an external 'phenomenal world' with uniform laws that gave a seemingly objective significance to that otherwise merely subjective pattern.

But then the sceptic's challenging question must simply be changed from why we should think that 'experience' is caused by an external world of roughly the sort in which we naturally believe to the question of why we should think this momentary pattern of mental content does deserve to be called 'experience'.

And indeed, Kant agrees that what he establishes to be true transcendentally is merely true among the presuppositions of experience; it is not true of the world as it is in itself.

What Kant needed was an explicit recognition of the a priori judgment that we all implicitly make, that, given the pattern of our experience, it is overwhelmingly probable that there exists, as a full reality, an external world beyond our present mental content, a world more or less of the sort in which we normally believe.

Sometimes what has been redefined in an effort to avoid scepticism is 'truth'. The trick is to lower the standard enough to allow us to reach 'truth' despite the sceptical nagging that this is impossible. The high standard requires for its truth that a belief or claim, if it is to be regarded as true, correspond with reality. The sceptic challenges our justification for thinking that there ever is this correspondence between our beliefs and an external world.

Theories concerning truth that are meant to disarm such scepticism by lowering what counts as truth are self-refuting because it turns out that they can make no sense except as claims that these theories themselves are true according to the rejected higher standard. But then they make no sense at all since it is essential to them that nothing can be true in the way that they would have to be.

One important example of this is pragmatism, the doctrine that beliefs are true if, and only if, they are useful. How is this thought to defeat scepticism? Well, according to pragmatism if our usual beliefs in an external world are useful then we can know them to be true despite any sceptical worries about whether such beliefs correspond to a world that is actually there.

But the pragmatist doesn't notice that this amounts to a self-refutation. Pragmatism can only be true in a way that it cannot allow. What brings this out is to notice that a pragmatist must hold that if a rejection of pragmatism became useful then that rejection would therein be true—but only because it was useful. Hence the pragmatist would still be regarding pragmatism as the underlying truth about truth quite apart from whether pragmatism was useful. In other words, pragmatism cannot see itself as true merely pragmatically.

Another important example would be a theory that insisted that the truth of what we say depends on nothing but rules for when it is right to say such a thing in our 'language game'. This insistence can seem to defeat skepticism because we usually allow ourselves to say that we know all manner of things to be true that a sceptic is maintaining we don't really know. (Of course, I've argued that this is because we *do* know these things.)

But it could make no sense for a holder of this theory to regard the truth of this theory as decided by the rules of a language game. For the view must hold that if a rejection of this language game theory itself were allowed by the rules of a language game then that rejection would therein be true—but only because it was in the rules of the language game to say that it was. Hence this theory would still be regarding itself as the underlying truth about truth quite apart from whether it accorded with our linguistic practices to say that it was true. And thus, it cannot be regarding its truth as fixed by the rules of a language game.

Part II of this book has, until now, been written in the style of a talk about empirical reasoning given to an audience. These final remarks are addressed more directly to you, the reader:

In this section, I have warned against the shallow move of defining 'humebird' as blue simply to ensure that the next humebird we see will be blue. (As though language could make a humebird blue.) I have suggested that many celebrated philosophical positions amount to little more than that sort of thing. Instead, we must engage with the world itself by thinking clearly about probability.

I anticipate that some philosophers, when faced with the improbability of your entire sperm cell–lottery history from your own perspective, may insist that the word 'I', used 'rigidly', designates that history—and so will treat your presence in the world as no more improbable for you than the use of the word 'I' to refer to yourself—or attempt some such linguistic manoeuvre. (As though our use of language had placed you in the world. This one's a bit like painting the centre of the target wherever the dart has landed.) But let's instead face reality by thinking clearly about probability.

32. What Universalism Is Not

Note carefully that interpreting what I am saying in universalism as anything like a redefinition of 'I' to meaning 'everyone else too' is simply a bad misinterpretation of universalism. That would indeed be exactly like redefining a 'humebird' as having to be blue in order to assure ourselves that the next 'humebird' we see must be blue.

Recall that what was required to solve the problem of induction in the humebird case was instead positing a deep, substantive and stable humebird character that made them blue while allowing in our mere use of the word 'humebird' that they not be blue. Well, universalism does not change what we mean by 'I'; it is a discovery, based partly on probability, of what I am.

Universalism is claiming that the existence of that deep, substantive and stable thing we each individually call 'I'—that thing whose existence gives me 1) my true presence in the world and 2) my self-interest—is due to the immediacy in my experience rather than the objective identity of just one of the human beings that I (also) am. This stability of my existence in immediacy I establish through many considerations—but never through a redefinition, a mere relabelling of distinct persons—when these are conceived of as having distinct presences in the world and self-interests—as 'me'.

Let me add that neither am I indulging in a sneaky equivocation between 'all experience being immediate for whatever has it' (with which my opponents can easily agree) and the substantive controversial claim that 'all experience being immediate is all experience being mine in the deepest sense of being mine'. My arguments, including the probability argument, are all of them for the substantive claim—that it is the immediacy of experience alone, and not merely one thing's having experience with immediacy, that gives me my very own presence in the world and self-interest.

If I would be truly present in the world only if some single distinct conscious thing had immediacy in its experience, universalism could not have overcome the improbability of my existence in the usual view. It is only that substantive overcoming—not the weak claim easily agreed with that all experience is immediate for whatever is having it—that makes the probability argument for universalism work. Only the substantive claim could turn the hard game of the usual view into the easy game of universalism.

Part III:
Using Our Empirical Reasoning to Establish the Truth of Universalism

I show that the logic of empirical discovery requires us to accept the radical view of what a person is. I then show how this change of view is essential for a thorough understanding of physics.

I shall now be carefully developing an immensely powerful statistical argument for universalism.

Part II was in the style of a talk. It will be convenient to open this part as a description of a talk.

1. CARDS: DEMONSTRATING THE PERSPECTIVAL CHARACTER OF PROBABILITY

I show my audience a deck of 52 cards and ask someone from the audience to step up and randomly draw a card from it. A card is drawn.

Then I point out that according to an extremely common way of thinking this event that had just occurred—the drawing of this particular card—has only the low probability of 1 in 52.

I then begin demonstrating the mistake of that view by having the whole deck of cards distributed, with each card going randomly to a different member of the audience.

Next, I have a single card drawn from another deck. I ask which member of the audience had received the corresponding card in the distribution of the first deck.

Somebody shouts out 'me', and I say to that person, 'An event has just occurred that is indeed improbable for you, with a low probability of only 1 in 52. The card randomly drawn from this deck has matched the card that you happened to receive in the random distribution of the other deck. So, for you, and you alone of everyone here, this event involved an improbable coincidence'. And I give to this winner a little prize—a small chocolate egg.

Finding Myself: Beyond the False Boundaries of Personal Identity
Special Supplement, *Midwest Studies in Philosophy*
https://doi.org/10.5840/msp202549Supplement6

But then I also point out to the others who had received cards in the distribution that this same event was instead a very probable event for each of them. For each of them the event must be described as the drawing of a card that did not match the one that was earlier received. For them it was an event with the high probability of 51 in 52.

And now I address those in the audience who happened not to have any card distributed to them. For you, I say, this same event had no improbability at all. It was just the event—guaranteed under the stipulated general circumstances—of some card or other being drawn. You had no horse in this race and neither won nor lost. You observed nothing improbable in this result. For you there was no coincidence. Oh yes, you could empathise with the winner and see that for that winner this was improbable.

When we standardly describe drawing a particular card as having the low probability of 1 in 52, we are implicitly putting ourselves in a perspective of designating just that particular card independently of whether it is drawn. And from that perspective the probability actually is only 1 in 52 that it would be the one drawn. But the event of just drawing a card with no independent designation can involve no improbable coincidence and therefore no improbability.

In other words, the probability appropriate for the uninvolved observer is not the probability of the single individual card, which would be 1 in 52, because that card has not been in any way highlighted, but rather the probability of the disjunction of all the individual cards—that is, all the cards separated by 'or'—which would be 52 in 52.

Someone objects, 'But the probability of a suit, like spades, is always greater than the probability of a particular card, like the deuce of spades. So, aren't those probabilities fixed non-perspectively?'

No. A match between a card randomly drawn and an independently designated suit (1 in 4) will indeed always be more probable than a match with an independently designated particular card (1 in 52). But the probability of just some suit or other being randomly drawn and the probability of just some particular card or other being randomly drawn, which are the only relevant probabilities from the perspective of the uninvolved observer, will always for that uninvolved observer be equal—both will be certain given that a card is being drawn. The disjunction of all 4 suits and the disjunction of all 52 cards have the probabilities 4 in 4 and 52 in 52.

Let's explore further the perspectival character of the probabilities in this sort of case. If only one person in the audience had been handed a randomly drawn card from the first deck instead of the whole deck being distributed to the audience and if then that one card had happened to match the one that was drawn from the second deck, that would be rightly considered an improbable coincidence by the whole audience. The singleness in the lecture hall of that first selection would have independently designated that card for all of us in the same way the winner's card being the only card that participant held had independently designated that card for that winner—but nobody else—in the first version, the full distribution.

But now imagine that there were many, many lecture halls in which this was happening and there was an observer technologically connected to all of them. For that observer there would be no improbability in roughly 1 in 52 of those lecture halls having a match. Such an observer could fully appreciate that in the perspective of all of us in this hall the matching of cards here was and would forever remain an improbable event. It was genuinely a local improbability. But nothing had singled out the hall for that observer independently of the matching. For that observer all the probabilities of all the attempts to get a match across those many lecture halls added up and made observations of winning halls extremely probable from that perspective. That observer's relationship to our win in the hall parallels the relationship of the non-participants within the hall to the winner among those receiving the distributed deck in that earlier version.

2. CARDS: DEMONSTRATING THE PERSPECTIVAL CHARACTER OF INFERENCE

Now let's switch to talking about an inference based on probability.

I have an antique safe here on stage into which I have already placed one of two possible things—either a single card or a whole deck.

I will next ask someone from the audience to select a single card from another full deck. I will then say whether the selected card corresponds to one that is in the safe. In the version of this called the 'easy game', it is the whole deck that is in the safe, thus making it easy to get a match. If I am playing the 'hard game' with you, then only one card is in the safe, making it hard to get a match. The evidence I am about to give you should allow you to infer which game is being played. That evidence is my now telling you that the card you have drawn from this other deck does indeed match a card in the safe. Do you think we are playing the hard or the easy game?

How should the reasoning go here? The evidence is that the cards match. The truth of the easy game hypothesis would involve no improbability in this result. But if the hard game hypothesis is true, then that evidence, the match, is an improbable coincidence. The only way the hard game hypothesis could be true, then, is for something that is improbable within that hypothesis to have taken place. But surely it is improbable that something improbable is what has taken place. So, the evidence requires the inference that it is improbable that the hard game is being played and that it is probable the easy game is being played.

Probability is perspectival, and therefore inferences like this one that are based on probability are also perspectival. It will be a step towards helping us to see this if we next think of either a hard or an easy game being played at once across many halls that are isolated from each other. In the hard game there would be but a single card in the safe of every hall while in the easy game there would be a whole deck in every safe.

Now add to this that there are as many outside observers as there are halls. Each is isolated in a cubicle with a screen; and each is guaranteed to see on the screen only a recording of a hall where the cards had matched—whether this is one of the infrequent halls in which a match occurred if it was the hard game that was played or one among the clean sweep of halls having a match if an easy game was played—in which case each of the halls will be seen by one of these observers.

Such an observer, guaranteed to see a match in either game, would see the audience in the hall on the screen rightly infer from their perspective the greater probability that the easy game was played but be wholly unable to join them in their inference precisely because such an observer had been guaranteed to see a match in either game. The observer's targeted perspective blocks the inference.

(Anyone worried about unknown prior probabilities here or elsewhere can find my discussions of that topic in Part II, sections 10–13 and Part V, section 23. In proto-Bayesian probability we recognise that any unknown prior probabilities probably favoured the hypothesis that made the evidence more probable. An overall hypothesis in which a bad hypothesis was favoured by the unknown prior probabilities would have required that something improbable happened either in the occurrence of a good hypothesis despite its being improbable or the occurrence of the evidence despite the bad hypothesis occurring. Of course, our confidence about the unknown prior probabilities should increase with the amount by which a good hypothesis favours the evidence more than a bad one.)

3. GETTING CLOSER TO THE BIG ONE

Let us now shape our probability thought experiments to lift them closer and closer to the inference to universalism. One thing will be to bring down a great deal the probability of winning a hard game. Another will be to focus once again on the individual winner. We'll also ditch the cards and make this into something more like a lottery.

Let's say I have a gazillion people in my audience. There are two games that might be played. In the easy game everyone in the audience is a winner and the prize each will win is vanishingly small. In the hard game only one participant has been randomly selected as a winner and the prize is very, very big.

Each audience member is given a sealed envelope containing inside it a slip of paper that will have written on it either 'winner' or 'loser'; and then each retires alone to a private cubicle. Please put yourself into this situation as one of the players. You open the envelope with fingers trembling and read the word 'winner'. Which prize will you be expecting to get?

Well, if the hard game (with the very, very big prize) is being played, the evidence you have—that you have won—must be for you a one in a gazillion, incredibly improbable event. Sure, *someone* is going to win even in the hard game. But it would be mathematically ludicrous to say, 'Then why couldn't it just have been me?'—as much as you might want to be thinking this. Sure, as I say, there will be someone winning in the hard game, but there is only one chance in a gazillion that *you* would be that particular someone. Not because it's you, but because any participant singled out for any reason other than actually being the winner—as would happen if the winner *as such* was presented to the world after the result—would have only that less than miniscule chance of being the winner.

If an outside observer who had been informed about the hard and the easy game was allowed to select at random one of the participants, as a random sample of how the game turned out, what would that observer have to think on learning that this random sample was a winner? That this accords only with the easy game having been played, with everyone being a winner so that a random sample is bound to be that.

And you are that kind of random sample for yourself. Or let's say that opening your envelope has revealed to you a random sample of the slips of paper in the game. A random sample in the easy game will for sure look like this. But I wouldn't bet that a random sample in the hard game would have 'winner' on it when there is only one of those in a gazillion.

If the hard game had been played, then something incredibly improbable from your perspective would have to have happened when you opened your envelope and saw 'winner'. But it is necessarily improbable that something improbable has happened. I'm afraid you are almost certainly stuck with the vanishingly small prize.

If the easy game is played, all gazillion players will be thinking this way if they are rational. And they will all have correct expectations regarding their prizes. If the hard game is played, all but one will see slips that say 'loser'. One in a gazillion will read 'winner' and be misled by still wholly correct reasoning to expect that it's the easy game. But there would have been only one chance in a gazillion of being misled by this reasoning in the hard game. And, of course, no chance at all of being misled by it in the easy game.

4. THE AWAKENING GAME—HARD OR EASY—
IN THE HOTEL OF COUNTLESS ROOMS

Please imagine next a hotel with countless rooms—and on the bed in each room a single occupant who is being caused to remain in a dreamless sleep.

In the easy game all these sleepers will be awakened. In the hard game only one random sleeper will be awakened. The rest will sleep forever.

You find yourself awake, and you are made aware of the two possible games.

You must infer that if these conditions apply it is overwhelmingly more probable that the easy game and not the hard game is being played.

Your evidence for this inference is that you are awake. One of the available hypotheses to explain this evidence, that the hard game is being played, would require this evidence, your being awake, to have been an unimaginably improbable occurrence, whereas the other hypothesis, the easy game, involves no such improbability. You are required by the basic logic that powers all our empirical knowledge to reject as absurdly improbable that the hard game is the one being played and believe instead that it's the easy game.

Of course, the incredibly rare awakener in the hard game would have been misled by this reasoning into preferring the hypothesis of countless awakenings, which would in that case have been false. But being asleep—and therefore in no condition to engage in a misleading inference—would have been overwhelmingly more probable in the hard game. Thus that the inference is not misleading must be, from the rare awakener's perspective, overwhelmingly more probable than that it is. (But an uninvolved observer, say, on a street outside the hotel, who was given a winner's name as being that of either one of countless awakeners or that of a sole awakener, could not use that information about that awakening to infer one thing or the other. That awakening if only one had been awakened would entail for this observer no improbable coincidence.)

Let's elaborate a bit on what I've just said parenthetically. Imagine two styles of observing the game from outside—a random sampling of just one among all the potential awakeners and an observation guaranteed to be of one who has awakened.

An external observer who could make a random observation of just one room would have to infer the immensely greater probability of the easy game if this random sample contained an awakener. The awakener in the game, from that awakener's perspective, is just such a random sample relative to awakening among the potential awakeners. (Let's make clear the equivalence in the ability to infer that the easy game is being played between two cases: 1) an external observer makes a random observation of a room and finds an awakener in it, and 2) a player observes having been awakened within the game. Suppose the external observer had randomised the observation by choosing the nearest room; being nearest would indeed be random relative to whether that room contained an awakener. Well, a player is likewise observing the 'nearest' room—the one occupied by that player. The randomness of the external observer's selection and the player's self-location are structurally equivalent, and so the inference to the easy game should be equally available in both cases.)

But an external observer who was simply guaranteed to be shown a winner either way—the one awakener in the hard game or a random awakener among the countless awakeners in the easy game—will not be able to make any inference. An awakener won't be evidence for that observer because there would be no improbable coincidence for that observer in seeing an awakener in the case of the hard game. This is a perspectival inference, open only to an awakener or an external observer with a random sample.

Before we now turn to proving the truth of universalism, it might be useful to remind you of a point at the end of the second part of this book about what universalism is not. Universalism is not a verbal manoeuvre, like redefining 'I' to mean 'everyone'. Just as we could not solve the humebird problem by declaring a humebird to be blue by definition, universalism does not seek to relabel distinct people in the usual view as 'me'. That could not possibly genuinely be of any help in making my existence more probable. (Nor would a relabelling of all the sleepers as 'me' have genuinely helped me to awaken in the hotel's hard game.) Universalism is rather a discovery of what I am. It claims that the deep, stable thing each of us calls 'I'—the source of my true presence in the world and my self-interest—comes from the immediacy of experience itself, not from the objective identity of one human being. And this is a substantive thesis, not the trivial observation (with which anyone would agree) that all experience is immediate for its subject. It is only this substantive claim about me that could make the probability argument for universalism work.

5. THE STATISTICAL INFERENCE TO UNIVERSALISM

You right now can observe that the world, whichever game it is playing, has awakened you to consciousness. The usual view of what you are—as I shall next make clear—is a hard game hypothesis if ever there was one. And universalism is the only easy game in town. The usual view must be rejected. Universalism must be accepted.

Just consider the history of begettings that would have been required for you to exist on the usual view of the matter. Let's say conservatively that during your conception there were 200 million sperm cells competing with each other to reach the egg first. And on the usual view if any sperm cell but the one that did happen to make it had got through to the egg instead you would never have been around (and never have had experience that was 'mine'). So, you had only a one in 200 million chance of being produced from that conception. But it gets far worse than that, because in order for that conception to have occurred, your parents had to have been conceived, and in each of their conceptions the chance of it turning out right for your later existence was, with our conservative estimate of the number of sperm cells, again one in 200 million. So, the chance of your emerging from those three conceptions was one in 200 million to the third power, which is one in 8 septillion—pretty slim. And, of course, all ancestral begettings before these had to be just the right ones for your future existence, the number multiplied in each preceding generation, and all of it going back to the time of the dinosaurs and far earlier than that. Otherwise it would have been eternally blank for you. You would have had no experience whatever. Only others would have been in the world instead.

That is the hard game that makes your evidence, that you exist, an absurdly improbable experience from your perspective. Universalism, by the most dramatic of contrasts, counts the sperm cell lotteries as wholly irrelevant. Your existence was not decided by the immensely demanding requirements for the identity of a human being; any such being would be you simply because its experience would necessarily have in it the immediacy that all experience has in it.

I want to press home further how improbable for you is your existence in the usual limited view of what you are. But first let me take a little time to deal with a pesky common mistake in thinking about such inferences.

When something is already there as our evidence, like the coin having landed heads a thousand times consecutively or you having found yourself to exist (and according to the usual view having had to win all the countless tougher than tough ancestral begetting lotteries), some people are tempted to think that the thousand consecutive landings of heads or your existence has now been endowed with a probability of one no matter how it may have come about, simply by virtue of our accepting it as evidence—as having already occurred. But that is a confusion.

What we are testing against the evidence are hypotheses regarding how the evidence came about. We accept that the coin has landed heads a thousand times consecutively, but that is hardly an acceptance of a fair coin being just as probable as a loaded coin to have produced that result.

A big box of coins has been dumped out on a floor, and every one of the hundreds of coins we can see has landed heads up. We know there were two boxes of coins—one full of only double-headed coins and the other full of only fair coins. It is madness to say, 'Since this has already happened, it is now certain that all the coins we can see landed heads-up either way, so we currently have no basis for deciding which of the two boxes this may have been'.

If the box was the one of fair coins, landing all heads was, is and always will be in any random single drop an improbable event. Within the fair coin box hypothesis itself, the evidence that we have would have been massively improbable to have occurred. And it always was, is and will be massively improbable that a massively improbable event happened, is happening or will happen. We can only rationally believe that such an improbable event has happened if its not having happened would have been even more improbable given other evidence. But that forced acceptance will not somehow digest away that improbability; and we will reject that hypothesis if the pressure to accept it somehow diminishes enough. Having already happened wouldn't make the improbable be probable.

We return now to appreciating the depth of improbability of your existence in the usual view and the corresponding degree of confidence we can have in rejecting that hypothesis as ridiculously improbable. Here is a fable, 'The Tyrant of the Sands', that may help us to feel the conclusiveness of such reasoning:

On the edge of the Sahara is a city ruled over by a cruel tyrant who plays a strange game with the life of a prisoner. First, the tyrant has a grain of sand dyed a colour sand would not normally be—a unique such colour for the prisoner. Next, a caravan is sent out to wander randomly in the Sahara for two weeks, where the grain of sand is released into a high wind. Another caravan is prepared when the first returns. In particular, a sticky substance is applied to just the tip of a hair at the very end of a camel's tail. The tail is loosely covered. Then this second caravan wanders randomly in the Sahara for two weeks till finally the tail is uncovered so that a grain of sand blowing in the wind may be caught on the tip of the hair. Only if this happens to be the same grain that was released by the first caravan will the life of the prisoner be spared.

Now, one time the second caravan returned with claims that the right grain of sand had been caught. The tyrant simply had everyone involved executed because this couldn't have been anything but a conspiracy. And how could he think anything else?

If there were countless Saharas, each with its tyrant of the sands, then some winnings of his game would be bound to occur; but, if you were a winner, that *you* happened to be one of the incredibly infrequent winners would have been precisely as improbable from your perspective as your winning if no more than that single game were ever played. So if you must choose between only two hypotheses, the hard game hypothesis and an easy game hypothesis in which it never matters to winning the game which grain of sand is caught on the camel's tail—in which all players are winners anyway—you must choose the latter hypothesis as enormously more probable to be true.

Yet fairly winning this tyrant's game would be a cinch compared to winning the game that, on the usual view of personhood, resulted in your existence. The number of grains of sand on all the beaches of earth is estimated at around 7.5 quintillion. I've already mentioned that the odds of you arising from three conceptions—your own, your mother's and your father's—are about one in 8 septillion. This, then, was like a game in which, by pure chance, you came up with just the right grain of sand among all grains of sand from all the beaches of over a million earths. But the need to secure all four grandparents before these three conceptions could occur makes the game immensely harder—with each of those four conceptions multiplying the odds against you by another 200 million.

Next, think of your luck continuing through each of thirteen generations' worth of distinct ancestors (counting in some earlier ancestral conceptions to make up for any overlap). Imagine all the atoms in the observable universe. Now let each atom unfold into its own universe. Count all the atoms in all those universes. Then let each of those atoms in turn become a universe. Perform this unfurling of every atom into a universe of atoms not just twice—but seventeen hundred times in total. The number of atoms at the end of this process would be a number over 136,000 digits long. That's some number! Printed out, it would fill thirty-two and a half single-spaced pages. At last, imagine an individual atom, chosen and hidden at random somewhere among all those atoms. Your chance of emerging from the thirteen generations would be as slender as, in one lucky dip somehow ranging equally across them all, retrieving just that single atom by pure chance.

So you must simply forget any such account of your existence. Winning the tyrant's game—a matter of capturing a grain of sand, without needing to distinguish between individual atoms, and confined to just the Sahara Desert—was indeed a cinch by comparison.

The only view that does not make your existence incredible, and that is not therefore (from your perspective) an incredible view, is that any conscious being would necessarily have been you anyway, that the logic of personhood has conspired to dye any grain of sand your winning colour. And how can you think anything else?

'But couldn't I just have been lucky?'

Well, it is not an impossible contradiction that the usual view be true and that your coming into existence was therefore the most incredible luck imaginable.

But you must, insofar as you are rational, regard it as overwhelmingly *improbable* that you were that lucky. It is on this *improbability* that I am insisting in this argument.

A variation on that question: '*Someone* would have existed on the usual view; couldn't that just have been me?'

Again, yes—that wouldn't have been impossible.

But—also again—you must regard it as overwhelmingly *improbable* that that lucky someone was you.

'Isn't there a "selection effect" that requires that anyone reasoning about this issue would have to be someone who had come into existence?'

Sure. And in the hotel only someone who was awakened could make the inference to the easy game there. Is this supposed to undermine either inference? How? Perhaps the questioner is thinking this selection effect can (magically?) turn whoever is existing, and therefore capable of making the inference, into you. Only universalism can do that—not magically but logically.

There are, in fact, two quite different kinds of 'selection effect'. One is a negative selection effect—the trivial restriction that only existents can observe, or only the awakened can reason. That explains nothing; it merely restates a tautology. The other is a positive selection effect—one that truly explains why this observation occurs and why it is not an event of extraordinary improbability.

Both hard games—the hotel selection of only one awakener and the sperm cell lotteries—impose the tough negative selection effect on those who will make the inference. If you are making the inference, you must have won a hard game. But that could not have made the winning of a hard game even the slightest bit more probable for you. Only a confusion between the player as you in particular and the player as whoever happened to win could turn that negative selection effect into something falsely seeming to have positively helped you to win a game so incredibly hard for you to win.

In both hotel and metaphysical easy games—by starkest contrast—the selection effect is the positive guarantee that you will indeed be in position to make the inference, because the required winning is itself guaranteed. The player as you in particular just automatically is whoever wins in those easy games—they positively pick you up and put you in position to make the inference—an inference that therefore should be to the overwhelmingly greater probability of this easy game having been played.

This contrast between negative and positive selection effects will reappear when we later consider the anthropic principle. There too, the negative effect—that one cannot observe oneself in a universe that does not produce consciousness—has no explanatory force. What matters is the positive effect we only have with universalism added: the guarantee that any universe producing consciousness will be observed by you. When that positive selection is combined with a multiverse that renders such universes probable, the reasoning is that of the easy games. Universalism puts you into an anthropic universe and turns what might otherwise seem a miraculous accident into necessity.

'Even if there is no coincidence for me in *my* existing, given the truth of universalism, isn't it still going to be somehow equally improbable that a particular *body* or a particular *mind* has emerged from a long line of begettings?'

No. Once you adopt universalism there is no longer anything coincidental for you in any such mere details of specific bodies or minds. If your awakening depended on a pre-specified pattern of heads and tails having been realised in one thousand tosses of a fair coin, then that pattern's realisation would have been a great, lucky coincidence for you. But if you would be awakened no matter which pattern came up, there is no coincidence for you in the pattern that did come up. Something's being improbable from your perspective would require such a coincidence.

There is the temptation of the sort I discussed earlier to think that there is always an improbable result when a fair coin is tossed one thousand times, because each possible pattern has only a one in two to the thousandth power chance of occurring. But, as we have seen, what this really means is that each possible pattern of heads and tails *designated independently of simply being the one that occurred* has only that slight chance of occurring in one randomly observed sequence of a thousand tossings. If we are merely reading off an actual result there is no coincidence and no improbability.

Recall that universalism and the usual view can agree on the conditions of body and mind that obtain in the world. They disagree only on where to draw the line between the essential and the incidental conditions for your existence. The usual view makes certain complex conditions of bodily or psychological identity essential requirements for your existence, while admitting that others, like the colours of your clothing, are incidental. Universalism puts all the conditions—other than that lone requirement of possessing a capacity for experience had with immediacy—on the incidental side of the line, along with the colours of what you are wearing. And if such demanding conditions as bodily identity are not required for you to exist, their realisation represents no coincidence or improbability for you at all—no more than do those colours of your clothing.

The inference to universalism is, like all probability inferences, perspectival. And in this case you could not be using what the usual view would regard as the existence of others as the basis of your inference. For from the single perspective you are supposed to occupy within that usual view, the production of others would not have been improbable, since, once you existed (which is the hard part), you would be in the position of simply seeing any winners there might be in the begettings of others. This would be a guaranteed observation for you of them but a random and therefore incredibly improbable observation of your own existence for you, but not for them. Universalism, however, puts you into the guaranteed observation position regarding all conscious organisms bar none. (There is no hard part.) For universalism, of course, makes it irrelevant to whether you and this experience exist what sperm cells hit what eggs. All experiencers would be you merely on account of the immediacy, the internality, the first-person character of their experience. So, you are always an awakener, and seeing yourself as an awakener, no matter what.

(What I say in the preceding paragraph about the existence of others within the usual view not involving improbability for you—and vice versa—is not strictly true. If you are an identical twin almost all your improbability of coming into existence would be shared by your twin. And to the extent you share ancestry with others—and at some very distant point in the past you share ancestry with everyone—you share also that much of your improbability and therefore that much of your basis for the inference to universalism.)

Even if the usual view, with its absurdly improbable requirements for one's existence, were true, it must have been wholly irrational for any conscious being existing to believe it. It would be like the one lucky winner in the hotel's hard awakening game rightly inferring the enormously greater probability that the easy game is being played. It would be, from an awakener's perspective, immensely improbable to be awake to be misled if the hard game is being played. And all conscious beings thinking straight about this must judge to be immensely improbable that they existed to be misled if the usual view of what they were was right instead of universalism.

By the way, I am being ridiculously generous to the usual view in focusing only on the sperm cell lotteries. For just one example, that view would regard precisely the same sperm cell lottery results as producing mere duplicates of us if the earth-like planet on which they occurred had been in another location, formed from different particular matter. Don't get me started!

6. THE HOTEL INFERENCE CHALLENGE

Can anyone rationally think that an awakened player could properly avoid inferring that the easy game is overwhelmingly more probable in the hotel of countless rooms? In my decades of discussing universalism, I have never come across anyone who thinks such avoidance is possible. (Since writing that, however, I have come across a partial holdout. In a recent YouTube video, my interviewer accepts that an external random sampler who finds an awakener in the sampled room should indeed infer the greater probability of the easy game—but somehow does not also accept that an awakened player could make the inference. I have accordingly taken the trouble, in the section of this book on the hotel inference, to add a little demonstration of the equivalence between an external random sampler and an awakened player in that respect.) I have discussed, through the years and in this book, various potential misunderstandings of the principles that underlie this hotel inference, but I am fully confident that nobody who simply understands the facts of the case (and intuitively recognises that the player is, in effect, randomly sampling a room) can deny that an awakened player should infer the overwhelmingly greater probability of the easy game with the awakening as evidence. An awakened player's inference seems to me about as unavoidable as 2+3=5.

So, then, if the hotel inference is unavoidable, can you find any relevant difference between the hotel inference and the inference to universalism that would make the latter inference avoidable? Regarding the inference to universalism people often do suddenly discover the problems they have regarding the principles of such inferences, most of which I have discussed. Showing how these same principles carry no difficulties in the hotel case can often be helpful.

A few people have highlighted the difference that the sleepers already existed in their hotel rooms before the game is played. I have never myself seen the relevance of that difference to making the inference to the easy game regarding personal identity; but one can, of course, simply modify the hotel case so that it is one in which the players would be altogether produced in the rooms instead of merely awakened. How could this not make the easy game of producing players in all the rooms more probable than the hard game of producing only a random one player?

There was an AI that told me in a chat that an 'actualist' could accept the hotel inference without agreeing to the inference to universalism because, while all the sleepers in the hotel would be actual, the possible people who do not get to exist in the sperm cell lotteries would not be actual. I replied that of course they wouldn't be actual. That's what everything turns on. But is that supposed to mean the actualist doesn't believe that you had to be lucky (like the awakened sleeper in the hard game) that the right sperm cell in your conception made it first to the egg? No, the AI agreed—you did have to be lucky. And with this the AI conceded that even the actualist actually couldn't duck the inference to universalism.

Let me here briefly point ahead to a new variation of the hotel inference at the end of Part V, where it is directly turned into an inference to universalism. In that version, you—an awakened player in the hotel—are now told with certainty that only you among the sleepers are awakened. But now you must choose between two metaphysical hypotheses that constitute, once again, a hard game and an easy one—the usual view and universalism. How could you not be compelled to favour universalism in those circumstances, as making this, your awakening, enormously more probable? And yet those imagined conditions are in every relevant respect like the conditions of your actual existence.

There's a way of bringing the hotel inference closer to the analogy of inferring that a coin landing heads a thousand times consecutively is not a fair coin, another inference that everyone accepts. (Though the interviewer I earlier mentioned said he'd need to examine the coin.) When I first published the hotel inference in 'One Self' it was a flipped coin version.

A fair coin landing heads a thousand times consecutively is indeed improbable. Yet it would be just as improbable if a thousand random fair coin flips had happened to match a single random list of heads and tails that had been written out before the flips. In my original hotel case, each of the countless sleepers had a different such list assigned to him or her. Then, for each sleeper, a fair coin was to be flipped a thousand times.

In the hard game the sleeper was to be awakened only if those coin flips had matched his or her personally assigned list (much like all the series of begettings having to go just right for you to come to consciousness in the usual view of personal identity). In the easy game everyone would be awakened no matter how the coin flips turned out.

Imagine you were awakened in one of the hotel rooms and it was explained to you that your awakening had resulted from one of those two games.

If I awakened and had that explained I would virtually know I was awakened in an easy game because it would have been ridiculously improbable for me that I had been awakened if that event required the fair coin producing by chance the strict pattern assigned to me.

Since there are countless sleepers in this story, there will be countless awakeners in a hard game too. Just much much much rarer. But each will be obliged to reason perspectivally, as I did, that the game was immensely more probable for him or her to have been the easy one. I technically could have been awakened in a hard game. It wouldn't have been an impossible contradiction. But it would necessarily have been immensely improbable for me that I would be awake in a hard game to be misled by this proper probability reasoning if such an improbable matching had been the requirement for that to happen.

I think you have no way of avoiding universalism.

7. FIELD OF WINNERS: A STARK DISPLAY OF HOW THE HOTEL INFERENCE IS PERSPECTIVAL

Once again consider the hotel inference case we have just developed, in which the hard game version made each sleeper's being awakened depend on a fair coin matching in a thousand consecutive flips a random list of a thousand heads and tails that had been pre-assigned to each sleeper whereas the easy game version had all simply awakened however the coins may have landed.

Let's add to this the twist that after the game is played all the awakeners in the hotel are instantaneously beamed from their rooms onto an unimaginably big field. The hotel had countless rooms with a sleeper in each; and therefore, even if the hard game was played, there would have been tons of winners. So, if you, as a player, found yourself in that winners' field you would be likely to see the same sort of thing whichever game had been played—a gigantic crowd around you as far as your vision could reach.

Notice now that you can use only one player's awakening to infer the greater probability of the easy game. The awakening of none of the others on the field could serve you as evidence for that inference.

This is because for you—and you alone—it would have been improbable for you—and you alone—to have won in the hard game. But each of the others in the crowd is being merely presented to you as someone or other who happened to be among the winners of whichever game was played. Their winning in a hard game was improbable in that same isolated way for each one of them but not for you.

And in the inference to universalism you could use as evidence only your own existence as being immensely improbable for you in the usual view but not the existence of others, who would be from your perspective merely those people who had happened to emerge from their sperm cell lotteries.

You had no dog in those races—only in your own. (As I noted before, this would not be strictly true in the case of this inference to universalism because of overlaps of ancestors, whose improbability for you of having come into existence would be shared with you by any of their other descendants. Such sharing of improbability would occur in the hotel as well if players there shared both the same flipping coin and the same list of heads and tails whose grossly improbable matching was needed to awaken them in the hard game.)

8. USING THIS SAME REASONING TO EXPLAIN THE ANTHROPIC PRINCIPLE IN PHYSICS

That the universe in its fundamental determinations conforms to what is needed for life to develop is called the 'anthropic principle'. Basic physics is anthropic (human-centred).

My favourite example of such agreement between physical law and the requirements for life is the strong nuclear force, which is one of the four basic forces of the universe. All protons are positively charged and therefore repel each other. How is it, then, that protons can stay firmly together in the nucleus of an atom? The answer is that one of the two nuclear forces, the strong nuclear force, attracts protons to each other more strongly than their positive charges repel them. But why, then, doesn't this stronger force, this attraction, pull together great heaps of protons? Well, it seems this force is stronger than the positive charges only over the very short distances within the diameter of a nucleus. It is a short-range force, whose strength falls off quickly, as the seventh power of the distance, unlike the long-range positive charges, whose strength falls off only as the square of the distance. One more question: why don't the protons that are within the nucleus, where the strong nuclear force is supreme, just keep pulling each other closer and closer? Here the answer is that the strong nuclear force has a strangely complex character; it suddenly becomes a repulsion when the protons get too close to each other. And so we have atoms, with positively charged nuclei holding round them negatively charged electrons—just what's required for there to be chemistry, and life.

If the basic features of matter that we see in this universe had resulted from purely a physical or mathematical necessity within the nature of matter itself—so that it could never have been any different anywhere, then such agreement between these features and the requirements for life developing would have to have been nothing but a stupendously improbable coincidence. But if matter instead were extremely protean, with its basic universe-wide characteristics varying radically across countless different universes, then no coincidence would have been involved in a miniscule fraction of these varied physical worlds happening to agree in such fundamental characteristics with what was required for life to develop.

Universalism must be added to a many-differing-physical-worlds hypothesis, however, before it can explain why our particular world did not fail to be amenable to life. On the usual view of a person, even if there are enough varied physical worlds to eliminate the coincidence of there *somewhere* in physical reality being an amenable universe, from the observer's perspective it would nevertheless be as great a coincidence that the *observer's* universe, that *your* universe was amenable, as it would have been if there was only one physical world and yet that was amenable to life. To eliminate the anthropic coincidence from our view, as rationality regarding the probabilities requires, we must loosen the conditions for personal identity, so that you, the observer, would automatically be in any of the universes in which the right conditions occurred. Then 'my' universe is guaranteed to be amenable. My universe will be every universe that is a host to consciousness. Only combined with universalism can a many-differing-physical-worlds hypothesis make probable the amenable character of *our* world.

Consider an analogy. You have awakened in a strange room from a drugged sleep. Three hypotheses attempting to account for your situation are offered to you.

First, that you were to have been awakened only if a single pre-designated number had come up on a single spin of a single roulette wheel with trillions of numbers on it. This is like the hypothesis of a single physical world that just happens to be anthropic.

The second hypothesis is that there were countless such wheels being spun, so that it was to be expected that the required number would come up on some wheel, but there were also countless sleepers, each assigned to just one wheel and awakening only should the right number come up on that one wheel.

Under these conditions, though it is probable there will be *some* awakening, in no way is *your* awakening, dependent still on just one wheel, made any more probable than in the first hypothesis. This, then, is like the useless combination of a many-differing-physical-worlds hypothesis and the usual view of identity, a view that would confine your existence to only one region of reality where one particular organism existed, a view that would regard even an organism just like you but in another world as not you but a mere duplicate of you.

The third hypothesis offered, the account you must accept as being overwhelmingly more probable than the others, is like the combination of many varied worlds and universalism. It is that any sleeper would have been awakened so long as the required number came up on any of countless wheels.

According to universalism I am any conscious being. Therefore, the existence of many varied worlds can make probable that some world will simply *become* mine by producing conscious beings. That world will, of course, have consciousness-producing natural laws; and it must be this combination of factors that actually is responsible for our experience of an anthropic universe. It is this, then, that gives us our physical laws. And accepting this points the way to understanding the fluid underlying nature of matter, of which the laws of our world are only one of a myriad of expressions.

There are two crucially distinguishable 'selection effects' that apply in our reasoning about the anthropic principle. There is a negative selection effect and a positive selection effect. The negative selection effect—that one can't observe oneself arising in a universe that does not produce consciousness—is useless at explaining why one's universe actually does produce consciousness. The positive selection effect—that one will observe any universe that produces consciousness—is indeed the explanation for one's universe producing consciousness when it is combined with a multiverse that makes the occurrence of such a universe probable. This positive selection effect is only there in universalism. Universalism is the lubricant that gets the multiverse solving the puzzle of the anthropic principle.

9. UNIVERSALISM AS A STAGE IN SCIENTIFIC UNDERSTANDING

But this universalist explanation of the laws of physics would come at the end of a long line of discoveries within those laws that were only made when other aspects of this same illusion were given up.

Here, as the place of my current experience, is always subjectively central for me. Yet, on account of my mobility, I can easily see through a pretension that this personal subjective centrality is in some way objective. The objective place currently here could so obviously have been there instead. Yet our general place, earth, was mistakenly viewed as at the objective centre of existence till reasoning and an increasing familiarity with what was beyond the earth brought informed people to see that this centrality too was only subjective. Getting past that illusion was essential to the Copernican and Newtonian revolutions.

The one-directional character of time does not allow us the sort of mobility we have in space. And time, unlike position, also seems not to allow for a distinction between a personal and a general one. The time that is now for me looks to be the same across the world. These factors make the illusion regarding now, that it is the objective centre of time, much harder to shake off than the similar illusion regarding here.

Yet when we imagine, as in at least a crude way we can, traveling in time with some of the freedom of our movements in space, we can easily see that any past or future time would simply be the present to any time-traveller who had arrived in that time. And we can do something similar to help us shake free of the illusion regarding who we are. We can imagine a kind of mobility in this too. That is what we were doing when earlier I asked you to consider all the changed conditions that would still leave your experience being 'mine'. If the first-person character, the immediacy of the experience remains (and how could it not in anything that could count as experience?), we can imagine a continuum of hypothetical physical and psychological differences in an experiencer that could in principle take us through all the objective and subjective conditions of all possible consciousness without the slightest change in the experience being mine and the experiencer being me.

What we are doing in this reminds me of Newton's famous cannonball thought experiment. He showed that the distinction in kind between the matter of objects on the earth, called 'terrestrial', and the matter of a distant body like the moon, called 'celestial', was false by asking us to imagine that a cannonball, clearly terrestrial, is fired repeatedly from a very high mountain with progressively greater velocities. At no stage is there any change at all in the sort of matter in the cannonball. Changes of velocity are in the wrong category to constitute changes from terrestrial to celestial matter. Yet, finally, there must be a velocity that will give the cannonball the moon's sort of motion around the earth. The relevant distinction between the matter of the earth-bound cannonball and the matter of the moon was one of circumstance and not of kind. And the same general laws of motion could therefore be discovered to be governing both.

The universalist view of time, as well as space, is already at the heart of physics. Relativity theory depends on letting go of an objective present time. I am arguing here that only an extension of this treatment of space and time to personal identity will allow us to solve the most fundamental problem of physics—discovering what is behind the laws of physics. To do so we must see that being here, being now and being mine are none of them due to exclusive objective conditions, as they seem to be, but rather to the universal subjective impression of immediacy in every experience of a place, time or organism. We must see that all places, times and conscious organisms are equally 'this one'. For a failure to see this must distort our view by forcing us to accommodate in it what seems to be our own special objective status; and that awkward accommodation must then ruin any prospect of discovering the truly objective universal principles that govern the world.

10. CONCLUSION OF PART III

A reversal of ordinary thinking gets us to considering that an experience being mine could be due to its inherent first-person character rather than to an objective identity of the thing that's having it. In this reversal of thinking, it is this inherent character that, making the experience mine, makes whatever is having it me.

Cutting loose from the constricting identity of a thing allows us to discover that the inherent character making experience mine would be there equally in all experience—thus making all things having all experience me. The confined reach of integrated mental contents would be what made it falsely seem that experience being mine was itself confined by the identity of the one thing having that small measure of integrated experience.

We explore the conceptual rightness of this reversal of ordinary thinking. We come to see the incoherence of limits to what I am in eternal recurrence, trading of parts between duplicates, variations in all sorts of properties other than the having of experience with the character of being mine and the experiencing of non-integrated experiential contents after brain bisection.

Next we see that a piece of evidence that I have in my own possession—my own existence—requires this reversal of thinking to make the observing of it at all probable from my perspective. Just as I would be required to judge, from the perspective of my own awakening (in a hotel with countless forced sleepers isolated in rooms), that my awakening had resulted from an easy game of all sleepers being awakened rather than a hard game with only one random awakening, I would from the perspective of having awakened to my own consciousness be required to judge that this resulted from the easy game of my identity being guaranteed by the character of experience rather than the hard game of only one thing that was me emerging from all the begettings of me and every one of the ancestors that were needed in the hard game for my begetting eventually to occur.

Throw in as well that making it at all probable from my perspective that I am in a physical world with fine tuning for the possibility of conscious life requires that I myself would have been awakening to consciousness anywhere in a multiverse that the required fine tuning had happened to appear (the easy game) rather than having my identity confined to just one physical world whether the fine tuning happened to appear there or not (the hard game). I can now explain the physical laws of my world.

All of this based on a simple shift in emphasis from a thing being me to an experience being mine.

11. WHERE DOES THIS POINT ME?

The concentration of this book—and certainly of this part of it—has been on showing the truth of universalism. But I have also said some things in the first introduction and in Part I about the personal implications of universalism, and I'll say some more now.

I want the best for myself. Of course I do. Any other motivation is absurd. So I urge my selves not to promote self-harming views of the implications of universalism.

For example, it will not do me good to believe, and to promote to myself,
the false view that the treasure of boundless experience is mainly horrific.
Though there certainly is a large measure of suffering—and terrible suffering—in the store of all consciousness, and though this can easily grab my
attention because I often usefully look for the problems in things, I can nevertheless expect most of my experience to be pleasurable and even joyful.
Living things are fashioned by evolution, or by God, to function well in their
environments. Consciousness, with its fascinating richness, is fashioned to
be attractive to its possessors, in order to keep them clinging to life. Only
life-clingers stay alive and reproduce.

(And I also should not expect any human distaste for other forms of
conscious life to carry over into what it is like for me when I am actually in
those lives.)

A fanatical attention to universalism that forgets to respect the power of
our many motivations based on the illusion of being distinct selves would be
a faulty basis for increasing my happiness. For example, I should deal subtly
and thoughtfully with mistaken desires for retribution. And I should ally myself with usual-view motivations, like sympathy, that can lend weight to the
actually appropriate motivation of self-concern.

The local effect of universalism should be to feel particular self-interested concern for that life, and the surrounding lives, one can actually influence.
It would be an awful mistake to think of that practical focus as somehow
swamped by the larger reality of all the consciousness beyond it that is also
mine. Simply do whatever you can for yourself in each of your situations.
Stick with each of these as long as you can to make it better. Treat each life
you live as precious—but also know that there is so very much more for you.

Use the truth of universalism to weaken, soften, and overcome the fear
of death, selfishness, group bias and desires for retribution and revenge. Use
it against the pain of thinking that life is permanently confined to disap-
pointment, or that the good in it is permanently limited by the death of one
organism.

Universalism could convert all who think rationally to a new self-interested dedication to the welfare of all humans of every group and other sentient beings of every species, present and future—all of them me, all of them
you. Those already campaigning for any aspect of that welfare should seize
hold of universalism as the surest motivating engine for improving it. What
a waste if such campaigners do not see that! The golden rule supercharged.

Part IV:
Further Considerations

I enter into further considerations. Topics include Nick Bostrom's objections to unification and how the radical view is related to Buddhism, dualism, Hume and Parfit.

1. ULTRA-INSULATING BUDDHISM

Is universalism really the only easy game in town? Very much so.

There is a sort of view that departs from the usual view by going in the opposite direction from universalism. The usual view imposes insulating boundaries on who I am that confine me within the life of a single human being. The rival view we shall now consider confines me to a much smaller momentary existence that does not extend beyond the present moment of a human being. And it thus makes my far more pinpointed existence even more improbable than that I have on the usual view.

In a Buddhistic view any psychological process would be forging on through a succession of non-continuous experiencers. At any point in this process there would be an experiencer with its momentary pains and pleasures, but it could have no non-illusory self-interest in any further accumulation of experience as this would not belong to it—since not that subject but only other momentary subjects would exist in any further experience. The experience would belong to no continuing subject. Neither self-interest nor other-interest (interest, that is, for the self-interests of others) would be appropriate.

But notice that this radical and bleak view does not escape either the conceptual or the statistical difficulties of the usual view of the person. For each such momentary subject would have its own identity conditions involving both a token and a type. There would arise the question of whether this momentary subject would have existed if its identity conditions had been divided or had been different by degree. And the improbability for itself of existing of any of the momentary subjects would make such a hypothesis statistically untenable just as it did the usual view of the person. For in every moment of the ongoing mental process an inference would be supported that

Finding Myself: Beyond the False Boundaries of Personal Identity
Special Supplement, *Midwest Studies in Philosophy*
https://doi.org/10.5840/msp202549Supplement7

from this momentary perspective the existence of this momentary subject would be overwhelmingly improbable by contrast with the existence of the universal subject in universalism.

2. THE IMMATERIAL SUBSTANCE VERSION OF THE USUAL VIEW

Some philosophers support a mental substance—simple, indivisible, immaterial—as a candidate for the self of personal identity. I've mentioned this, but I'd like to say a bit more about it here.

This version of the usual view is as vulnerable as the materialist one to both conceptual and statistical objections.

For one thing, the appearance in the world and the fate of a mental substance would be dependent on the identity of the physical organism whose self it was supposed to be. If, for example, an embryo had split into twins, the different identities of the products would have required distinct such mental substances to be assigned to each, as the two selves of the twins. In all the possible lines of begettings there would have been countless such possibilities of distinct mental substances—the overwhelming majority, of course, never appearing in the world. That those conditions to which your mental substance would be attached arose in the world and that you were not instead among the countless possible mental substances that on such a view will never exist must be an incredibly improbable coincidence for you.

The results of splittings would be as paradoxical as ever if we conceived of them as occurring in association with a mental substance. Consider how after brain bisection there seem to be two subjects where before there was one. How are these two subjects related to the original mental substance? That original substance would have survived with either hemisphere if a stroke had wiped out the other. But can it now be with both? Can it be with neither? Can it be with only one or the other? And if we imagine gradual changes from, say, your bodily and mental conditions to mine, when does your mental substance disappear in favor of mine?

Note carefully that I am not here arguing against dualism as a position on the mind-body problem. I am only arguing that if there are mental substances the identity of the person depends only on the immediacy in the experience had by the mental substances and not on the identity of a mental substance itself.

3. HOW ABOUT A SINGLE SUBSTANCE?

Could we not say that there is but one self and this one self is a single substance somehow existing equally in all experiences? This universal substance view, however, solves neither the conceptual nor the statistical problems of the usual view. There is in it, in fact, a further, much more obvious conceptual incoherence and a much greater improbability. Merely asserting that one substance is somehow present at once in all experience does not make it understandable how this could be or what it could mean. (By contrast the quality of immediacy is naturally present in all experiential content, as anyone must admit. How all experience could be mine and now if this depended on nothing but this natural quality would be no mystery.)

And the improbability of your existence must be even greater than in the usual view if it depends on the existence of a single substance that is somehow the only one allowed to exist. Think of the countless other such substances, *all* of which will not make it into the world on such a view. You would have been required to have been luckier on this hypothesis than on any other. (If, however, something in the very logic of experience, the presence in it of an inevitable quality, ensures that any conceivable subject of experience possesses all of experience, then the improbability for a subject that it exists has been therein eliminated.)

Let me clarify this further. If the view is that it is logically necessitated that there could only be one substance in the world (whether this substance is both physical and mental or—in an idealism—only mental), what is it that resulted in this substance being you instead of somebody else? Its singleness as a substance and the supposed logical necessity of that singleness cannot somehow make it you. And if the answer is the universalist one—that its immediacy of experience makes it you—then the substance being single is irrelevant to its being you.

4. A HUMEAN BUNDLE OF PERCEPTIONS

Hume's empiricism regarding the origin of ideas was so strict, at least in some of his writing, that he rejected the possibility of entertaining any idea of any possessor of the perceptions in his mind. All ideas, he thought, were derived from and therefore limited to being of perceptions. The mind, in his only legitimate idea of it, was nothing but a bundle of perceptions, without them being possessed by anything.

Let me make use of this restricted idea of the mind to bring out once again the way that universalism focuses purely on experience being mine through its quality of immediacy and not at all on a thing that may possess that experience. (Yet let me point out that we need not feel constrained by Hume's empiricism in our discussion.)

According to universalism, if the world contained nothing but a Humean bundle of perceptions, with no thing as a subject possessing them, then those perceptions, purely on account of their inherent immediacy, would be mine and I would therein be present in that world in the centrally important way.

What would I then be? I wouldn't be the perceptions themselves. They would be mine, not me. I'd be a fictional something from which the lines of vision were seeming to lead. And even though nothing was really there in that world but the perceptions, I would have full self-interest in diminishing any pains in the bundle and be present in the world—merely because an experience was mine.

And if instead it was true that some sort of thing actually was there, from which the lines of vision were leading, then that thing would be me, we could say, but that would be at bottom incidental to my proper existence and my personal experiential fate.

Furthermore, if that very same thing had been there but without any potential of having experience that was mine, it could not in any way have been me.

5. NATURALISM (DEREK PARFIT'S VIEW)

Consider a philosophical view about personal identity that I shall call 'naturalism'.

The naturalist sees that in the usual view there is an uneasy union of the complex conditions of a particular body or mind with the simple conditions of a subject of experience.

The naturalist sees the complex conditions as in themselves natural and unproblematic but doesn't see, as does the universalist, that the indivisibility and all-or-nothing presence of the subject of experience are also natural and unproblematic because they are simply features of the natural quality of immediacy that permeates all experience and determines personal identity.

The naturalist believes rather that only the positing of a supernatural simple substance could satisfy these seemingly non-natural properties of a person in the usual view and therefore proposes to purge the usual view's person of its non-natural component. And thus, for the naturalist, the person—or what is left of the person—is *merely* a complex natural process. A philosopher who, like Derek Parfit, thinks that what matters most in this is a *mental* process, rather than the physical process of the body, could be called a '*psychological* naturalist'.[1]

Parfit readily admits that he is running counter to the usual view by denying that a person's existence is an all or nothing affair. If a person's existence, as Parfit claims, is determined by the reach of connected memories

---

1.   Here I am only addressing Parfit's position in his early paper 'Personal Identity'.

and intentions, then this naturalistic identity, as Parfit admits, may change by degree.

Hence, if a year from now a person carrying on from me has only a certain fraction of the memories and intentions I have now, that person would be only by that same fraction's worth identifiable with me now. And the strength of my appropriate self-interested concern with that person's fate presumably ought to be measured as this same fraction.

One great problem with this view is that it seems we must on *any* view consider a person to be one and the same in all the integrated memories and intentions existing *at a single time*. Thus, if some person existing a year from now is to be identified *partially* with me because some of that person's memories and intentions carry on from mine now, since it must be one and the same person in all the integrated memories and intentions *at that time*, that person must also be identified *wholly* with me.

That person couldn't be me in thinking something that would be familiar to me now and at the same time be someone else in having an accompanying thought that would not now be familiar to me. It seems rather, contrary to Parfit's contention, that either all or none of those thoughts in the later stage will have to be mine.

Parfit tries to deal with cases of human fission, like brain bisection, by dropping any claim that the resulting branches of a split are identical to the original person and speaking instead of a 'survival' of the person in both branches. This would be like a plant surviving in all the plants that grew from its cuttings though it would not have been identical with any of them.

But when we try to think of the significance of such survivals to the original subject of experience, we find that the key question of future self-interest is every bit as puzzling as when we were struggling with the question of identity.

If one of your survivals was going to be dragged to a torture chamber and the other escorted to a wonderful party, how ought you now to anticipate such survivals? Will one, both or none of these two lines of experience be immediate for you like your experience now? Surely only the answer to this question can give us the proper basis for judgments of self-interest. And this is the ineradicable question of the identity of the subject of experience.

But Parfit claims that what is properly *important* to me is not personal identity but rather merely the survival of my memories and intentions. Let's look at this claim.

Imagine I learned that all the pattern of brain traces on which my memories and intentions depended would be recorded just as they were in the last moment of mental soundness before my death and later imposed on what had been somebody else's brain in place of its previous such patterns. That future person would then think just like me that 'this is me, Arnold Zuboff'. But would that person be right in thinking that? Would this then actually be me or would it be somebody else with memories just like mine, a sort of engineered clairvoyant?

Notice that it *could* be important to me that my knowledge and intentions be carried forward even if I think I am no longer to be in the world. Since that future person will at least be a bearer of my projects, the continuance of them in someone else could be important to me as might be the carrying out of provisions in my last will and testament.

But the way in which my self-interest could be *relevantly* involved in this case would have to be based on the additional factor of whether this future person would be *me*.

For example, imagine that I could at some time prior to that death, whose finality for me we are now trying to determine, hide away some of my wealth where only that future person with my memory traces would know where to find it. But, let us say, it would be a lot of trouble for me to do this hiding of my wealth.

If I think of that future person as being *me*, I have the *relevant* kind of self-interested reason for going to that trouble—that the future benefit will, like the present trouble, be *mine*. The two experiential contents, of trouble and benefit, will both come to *me* and the trouble for me may thus be over-balanced by the benefit for me. (Of course, by the way, universalism says I should have precisely such concern for all experience.)

If I think of that future person as another, however, any self-interested concern that may remain cannot be of this relevant sort. I could be pleased with the thought that this person will use that wealth to further causes in which I am interested whether that person will be me or someone else. But I cannot myself look forward to the pleasures that the wealth may bring that person in the self-interested manner relevant to the issue of personal identity if I do not believe that I will *be* that person. These are vitally different ways in which a future can be important to me, but only the latter is connected directly with the judgment about personal identity.

Now, intentions and memories and the carrying forward of projects are important only because there are persons, subjects of experience and self-interest, by whom they are experienced and for whom they have consequences. If I care about others, I care about the self-interests of others.

Furthermore, many things can be important to a subject of self-interest or someone else concerned about that subject independent of continued possession of any such memories or projects. It may be a goal of such a project to provide comfort for such a subject at a time when current memories and intentions will be lost, as in senility. If I became a victim of nightmares in which the view of myself and the world was violently altered, it could be of enormous importance to me or one concerned about me that the terrors in those discontinuous episodes be lessened if that is possible.

Carrying through with projects is important and being in the world as a subject of experience is important; but that doesn't make them the same thing. And in a certain respect the more basic of the two is being a person in the world. For projects without persons are meaningless.

Does it make any sense for Parfit to be calling 'persons' those beings whose identities or survivals are conceived of by him as determined only by the identities or survivals of their psychological processes?

We've already seen that the divisibility and changing by degree of such a process would make an essential connection between it and a proper subject of self-interest paradoxical. Perhaps the most consistent position like Parfit's would recognize itself as a straightforward rejection of both continuing persons and continuing self-interest altogether (and Parfit gestures sometimes at something like this radical solution). The view would be that there really exist only natural processes, that these processes embody an illusion that there are also, associated with them, continuing indivisible, all-or-nothing subjects of experience and that only these illusory, non-existent persons could be the proper subjects of self-interest (or other-interest).

This bleak view, it seems to me, turns out to be equivalent to the super-insulating Buddhistic view that I described earlier. There would, after all, still be consciousness accompanying the process (insofar as it was consciously carried on). There would therefore at each momentary stage of the process be at any rate a momentary subject of experience and self-interest, which would, for example, be that which was hurt if there was pain. But there would be no such subject of experience and self-interest somehow stretched out through the continued existence of the process.

Anyway, whether Parfit tries still to identify a person with a continuing process or lets the person fragment into momentary subjects of experience, the improbability for itself of existing, either of the process-'person' or of any of its momentary subjects, would make such a hypothesis statistically untenable just as it did the unreconstructed usual view of a person. For every moment an inference would be supported that the existence of *this* momentary subject, or *this* process-person, was from its perspective immensely improbable and should be given up in favour of the existence of the universalist subject of experience.

6. 'SOMEBODY UP THERE LIKES ME'

Let's briefly consider an attempted objection to the probability argument for universalism that I have encountered a few times. The claim of this attempted objection is that there is a version of the ordinary view of personal identity in which your existence would not have been improbable.

What if God happened to like you in particular—or God in some way needed you in particular for his plan? Wouldn't that have made it probable, or better than probable, that you were brought into existence?

There are a few problems with this hypothesis as a way of making your existence probable.

First, the game of being favoured by God would have been unbelievably hard to win—just like any other version of the usual view. He would have had to have favoured your existence more than the existence of all those countless potential people that do not get into existence given all those sperm cell lotteries (which are presumably rigged by him).

This is something like thinking it would be more probable that any lottery you won had been rigged to favour you rather than having been fair. Unless there is some independent reason to think that you would have been favoured by the riggers, that they favoured you would involve the same improbability as winning the lottery fairly.

But, someone responds, in my hypothesis I specify that I was the one favoured by God or I was the one favoured by the lottery riggers. Doesn't that specification make my existence or my lottery winning a probable event? Surely, in fact, that specification in my hypothesis is enough to make it certain I exist even without universalism being true.

I reply that this is no better than specifying that chance favoured your existence or chance favoured your lottery winning or specifying that a fair coin by chance had landed heads a thousand times consecutively when the evidence is a thousand consecutive landings of heads. These would be merely ad hoc specifications of the evidence having occurred within general hypotheses that by their general natures must have made that occurrence of the evidence improbable.

In proper empirical reasoning there is a 'precedence of the general' in which the general nature of an available hypothesis, like that of universalism or a loaded or double-headed coin, matches the general nature of the evidence, like you having come into existence or a coin having landed all heads a thousand times consecutively. A narrow, improbable, arbitrary ad hoc path having to connect the general nature of a fair coin or the usual view of personal identity to the evidence—all heads or your existence—must be useless for making the occurrence of that evidence other than improbable within the hypothesis.

Yet another problem with the 'Somebody up there likes me' hypothesis is that it misses what we are concerned about when we are thinking about personal identity. If there is a God making plans for the world, surely his interest would attach to the characteristics of the people whose production he brought about.

If he favoured putting a Moses in the world, for example, a precisely resembling twin in place of Moses would have done just as well. Yet within the ordinary view of personal identity a twin would have been a distinct person, with a distinct self-interest and presence in the world. God could not have had any reason to favour your existence rather than that of any of the countless potential twins of you that he might instead have caused to be produced.

(In universalism, of course, Moses, Pharoah, every less eminent Hebrew and Egyptian, God himself if he is a conscious thing, and the writer and every reader and hearer of this passage, would necessarily simply be you on account of the immediacy of its experience.)

7. BOSTROM AND UNIFICATIONISM

When in this book I discuss precise duplicates across the universe, I argue that not only the same person but also numerically the very same experience would be existing in every place and time that exactly such experience came into being. The experience of reading this discussion that you are now in—with all its great detail of sensation, thought and so on—is existing equally in each and all of the times and places in which just this same pattern of experience has been produced.

The analogy I drew earlier in this book is that not only the same character, Ishmael, but also the very same adventure exists equally well in every copy of the novel *Moby-Dick*. The identity of an experience from within that experience, like the identity of a novel prepared for its readers, is dependent on a repeatable pattern and not on the objective context that produces an instance of the experience or on those circumstances that figure in the particularity of a copy of the novel.

In this book I argue for this view using various thought experiments involving precise repetitions of episodes of experience and exchanges of quarters and halves. I also recount the 1961 thought experiment presented in my 1990 paper, 'One Self: The Logic of Experience'. Nick Bostrom, in his 2006 paper, 'Brain-Duplication and Mind-Duplication', bases his discussion of my view primarily on what I say in that paper.

Bostrom says that he is putting aside what he admits is an interesting question of whether the person would be the same across such duplication and will challenge only my contention that in such a case the experience would be the same. He calls my claim of the sameness of the experience 'unification', a name for my view that I have adopted in this book. (I thank him for that terminology.) The rival view that he argues for he calls 'duplication'.

For me all the occurrences are but a single unified experience, much as any number of copies of *Moby-Dick* would still be only the one novel, whereas for him each added occurrence would constitute more, further experience, even though each would be qualitatively identical to the others. Qualitatively identical but numerically distinct, like duplicate cups being produced by a factory.

In the paper 'Moment Universals and Personal Identity' (1978), also mentioned by Bostrom, in which I argue for unificationism but not for universalism (which I did not discover till 1983), I give this illustration of the significance of unification: If 'someone is offered a choice between a very pleasant experience to be precisely repeated a dozen times and a slightly more pleasant one to be had only once, he will do well to choose the latter'.[2] On my view the twelve precise repetitions would be only one experience. On Bostrom's view each would be yet more added experience. For me it would be as though someone was offered a choice between twelve copies of the same novel and one copy of a slightly superior one. For Bostrom it would be as though someone was offered a choice between twelve nice cups and one only slightly nicer one.

Let me say here a few things in response to what Bostrom is saying in his paper.

To begin with, I find it odd that he never directly answers my argument for unification, the 1961 thought experiment that involves the instantaneous exchanging of more and more parts of duplicate brains while the experiential stream in each brain remains qualitatively the same. In my 'One Self' paper these are precisely identical brains on either end of a long table being induced with electrodes to have exactly the same pattern of experience.

If, as he wants to say, there are two streams of experience, where is each after an exchange between the brains of equivalent quarters? It cannot have switched places in an exchange of only a quarter. And it cannot, as a seamlessly unified experience, be then only three-quarters the same. It must be wholly in the same place—and therefore, through a repeated application of the same reasoning, it must stay in that same place after each of the remain-

---

2.   Arnold Zuboff, 'Moment Universals and Personal Identity', *Proceedings of the Aristotelian Society* 52: 144–145.

ing quarters have been exchanged one by one. Yet the ultimate four-quarter exchange is an indistinguishable result from simply picking up the brains and switching their places, after which we'd swear that the streams must have changed places along with the brains. Bostrom just asserts that there are two distinct streams of experience throughout (based mainly on two unrelated arguments that I'll soon discuss); but he says nothing about where these streams are located or with which brain each is associated in the various stages of the thought experiment.

And as well as not considering my argument, Bostrom does not consider my analogy of the novel. (Think of exchanging equivalent parts of two copies of *Moby-Dick*. The same developing adventure is simply in both copies equally at any stage, just as I am claiming to be true of the stream of experience in the two brains.)

What Bostrom does do, however, is raise two very interesting problems that arise only if unification is combined with the universe being infinite (or anyway big enough for there to be extremely many precise copies of experiences), one problem having to do with value and the other epistemology.

Here is his problem for value: It is central to our values (as they currently are) to try to diminish suffering. But this would be rendered pointless if every possible experience of pain had been produced in a world big enough for this to happen—and therefore numerically the very same experience of pain whose occurrence we are trying to avoid will anyway exist. Yet, if not unification but rather Bostrom's duplication thesis is true, the avoidance of local occurrences of pain will still succeed in diminishing the total amount of painful experience and our ethical efforts will still have their point.

I agree with Bostrom that such an alarming effect on our calculation of values would be forced on us by accepting a combination of unification and an infinite (or big enough to be worrying) amount of experience production. But I am totally bewildered that he seems to think that the threat of such an upset to our current estimation of values can in any way settle the truth or falsity of that combination of unification and largeness. It might be nice if Santa Claus existed, but that doesn't help to settle whether he does. The real value of things depends on what they are, not the other way around.

Bostrom's epistemological consideration seems to me similarly askew. He points to a frustration of our accurate discovery of facts, if unification is true, since so many more experiences of error would exist than experiences of accuracy. Employing this consideration against the truth of unification sounds to me like yet another attempt at having desirability settle truth.

But this epistemological worry, unlike the worry about values, connects with a proper probability argument that I have sometimes made against the infinity—or worrying largeness—of life production. (The success of this argument against a too-big world, by the way, would of course also rid us of the too-big world's disturbing value implications.) It is closely akin to the argument in the second part of the 'One Self' paper against the identity of the subject of experience being defined by the specific content of its experience.

Here is the argument: If the experience-producing world is too big, a balance would have been tipped so that the most frequently occurring experience types, which are reflective of the reality that produces and shapes them, would have been flooded out by less frequently arising but far-greater-in-their-possible-number chaotic experience types. And if unification was true, since precise duplication could not increase the amount of experience, the greater frequency of reality-reflective experience in such a world could not increase the probability of one's current experience being of the reflective type rather than chaotic. Thus, it would have to be grossly improbable that this experience you are having was not chaotic. To relieve this improbability, one would need to let go of either unification or the excessive largeness of experience-producing reality.

Bostrom also says something that puzzles me, about odd relationships between events being required for unification to be true. I am encouraged by what he says to think that he hardly understands my view at all.

He says, 'If Unification were true, your brain may suddenly start to produce phenomenal experience at 10:32 pm tonight, having for the first time chanced into a state that happens not to be instantiated anywhere else in spacetime. And then, at 10:34 pm, it might just as suddenly cease to produce phenomenal experience as it enters a sequence of states that has already been instantiated somewhere else.'[3] If the unification I argue for is true, the experiences in question exist equally in all places and times in which they are produced. There is certainly no external metaphysical referee deciding which one is in some sense really having the experience. If all but my one copy of *Moby-Dick* were somehow suddenly to disappear, there wouldn't then magically occur an event in my copy of suddenly starting up as being the novel because other copies had given up the chore. The key relationship involved in the unification I argue for is the purely logical relationship of precise similarity in a certain regard, like my having the same number of pennies in my pocket as the number of planets going around some distant star. If a penny falls out the relationship may cease, but there's no pseudo-causal connection needed to mark the change. Notice also that in Bostrom's scenario I am located in only one particular position in spacetime, yet somehow my experience

3.   Nick Bostrom, 'Quantity of Experience: Brain-Duplication and Degrees of Consciousness', *Minds and Machines* 16(2): 188.

is still unified with that of others (or weirdly only starts when theirs leaves off?). But my understanding of unification includes my identity as whatever is having the experience. I am the character that exists in every copy of the novel.

8. A PROBABILITY ARGUMENT FOR UNIFICATION

There is a probability argument for unification. If instead the duplication theory were true, then certain objective conditions—like the objective particularity of the organism having the experience and the objective time and place of an experience—would have to figure into differentiating this experience you are in from all actual and potential duplicates of it. But that would make it immensely improbable from within the perspective of this experience that it would ever be existing. Yet it is existing, and so it must be within it judged to be immensely improbable that the strictures of the duplication theory do apply to it.

See the next part of this book, Part V, for much more discussion of the probability of the occurrence of this experience you are now in. The argument I've just given is a more specific version—concerning duplicates—of the more general argument developed in that next part against the 'objective individuation of experience'.

And in the final part of this book, Part VI, there is a thought experiment involving a million precisely similar disembodied brains—each of these brains, by means of radio transmission, interacting in a precisely similar pattern with the single un-brained body of the Part VI reader.

The question is posed to that reader of whether this would be a million precisely similar but nevertheless distinct experiences of that reading or else just one experience of it. This is, of course, the opposition between Nick Bostrom's 'duplication' and my 'unification' (but there, in my discussion of this thought experiment, referred to as 'the token view' and 'the type view').

When the reader is then informed that all but a random one of those brains have now been shut down, the reader has to judge that unification is much more probable to be true than duplication because duplication would have made it so much less probable that the reader's current experience of reading, which is serving as the evidence in the inference, would then be existing.

And then this same reasoning is applied to the experience of the reader as it actually is apart from the thought experiment. If Nick Bostrom's duplication view were true, how staggeringly more probable it would have to have been, from within the experience's own perspective, that the experience the reader is in right then had never come into existence—even if a precisely similar content had happened to exist (but, according to Bostrom's duplication, as the content of a distinct experience).

(The Part VI discussion of this million-brain thought experiment, unlike this section's discussion of it, attends centrally to the sameness of the *haver* of the experience.)

Here is an additional probability argument for unification:

My very good friend Jason Resch has pointed out that there are immensely more possible experience types in human-like complex consciousness as compared with much simpler ant-like consciousness. This can be calculated easily based simply on the vastly greater numbers of nerve cells (and their possible firing patterns) in things like humans compared to things like ants.

He goes on to say that this immensely greater number of possible human-like experience types in a reality containing enough conscious life so that a big proportion of ant-like experiences would be duplications would dictate that there is a greater probability of one's sample of experience being human-like rather than ant-like—but only within the unification view.

If one instead adopted the duplication view, the vastly greater number of individual occurrences of experience in ant-like things—counting (as a duplication adherent would) all the duplications as additional experiences—would overwhelm the number of occurrences of experience in human-like things and make one's evidence, which is having human-like experience, much less probable than having ant-like experience.

This point constitutes a statistical argument that, given one's evidence of an experience sample that is human-like, unification is immensely more probable to be true than duplication. If duplication were true, a sample of experience like this one would much more probably be ant-like than human-like.

And this argument, when combined with the argument in the previous section against a too-large life-producing reality if unification is true, might also be a basis for a very rough estimate of how large life-producing reality is likely to be given the truth of unification. It must be large enough to make the human-like experience types predominate over the ant-like types and yet small enough not to flood out the nature-reflecting experience types with more chaotic types.

9. THE ORIGIN OF THE SLEEPING BEAUTY PROBLEM

In the next part of this book, I will be arguing for universalism from an angle that starts in solving the Sleeping Beauty problem. I will very briefly describe the origin of the problem in the next part, but I think it could be helpful to describe in more detail here how that origin was involved with the development of universalism.

The Wikipedia Sleeping Beauty problem article says, 'The problem was originally formulated in unpublished work in the mid-1980s by Arnold Zuboff (the work was later published as "One Self: The Logic of Experience")'. This is roughly right. I sent an early draft of 'One Self' to Peter Unger, and he sent it on to Robert Stalnaker because I describe in the last section of the piece an encounter with Stalnaker in 1974 that had influenced my thinking about such matters.

As a new lecturer in the UCL philosophy department, I was giving a talk to the faculty that Stalnaker, then visiting London, happened to attend. It was a talk about the anthropic principle. When I came across that (at that time) obscure issue as an undergraduate in the late 1960s, it occurred to me that one could reason about it using probability.

Can I, as an observer of the (seeming) fine tuning of my universe in accordance with the requirements for life, infer that my universe is just one of countless universes varying in their fundamental physical characteristics (in what we now call a 'multiverse')? That multiverse hypothesis could banish the improbable coincidence there would otherwise be if there instead existed just one kind of physical world—the coincidence in that single-physical-world hypothesis between the basic physical laws that obtain throughout the universe and the requirements on them to allow the eventual development of complex chemistry, life and consciousness. (Vary by small amounts the strengths or other determinations of the four forces or the sizes, charges or other complications of the basic particles and there could have been none of that eventual development of complex chemistry and life.)

Stalnaker rightly objected, in a long discussion we had after my talk on this, that a multiverse would not in the least have improved the chances of specifically my universe being anthropic. His example was my playing a particularly tough version of Russian Roulette with almost no chance of survival. If I had survived I could not use that as any kind of evidence that there must be loads of such games being played, even though that would have increased the probability of somebody or other surviving in some game (that would very, very probably, however, have been other than mine).

About five years later I suddenly realised that the multiverse hypothesis had to be combined with a loosening of requirements in personal identity that, as it happened, I had been working towards in my thinking about that seemingly unrelated area of philosophy starting in my teens. If it would have been somehow guaranteed that any survivor of a Russian roulette game was equally me, then the hypothesis of countless such games being played rather than only one would easily banish the improbability of my observation that I survive in such a tough game. And if I myself would have been any and every observer, in a various enough multiverse, that showed up, as any observer would have had to do, in a rare anthropic universe, there is no improbability at all for me in specifically my universe being anthropic.

In my loosened view of personal identity—'universalism'—what makes a thing me is merely that its conscious experience has a first-person style, has immediacy—the pains really hurting, etc. That is the only basis of my being present in the world and of my having self-interest. It is how you are finding which conscious thing you are right now. Not with an objective checklist of facts but by being, as it feels, the 'only one' whose experience is first-person and immediate. But all experience is actually just like that. (By the way, if you are wondering how my being all conscious things could have escaped my notice, think about it. If I am all conscious things, I would in the case of each distinct occurrence of me have the strong illusion of my being only that one conscious thing—on account of the non-integration across conscious organisms of the contents of their experience. It would be the same illusion of being a less extensive experiencer than I actually am that would occur in brain bisection.)

I then soon generalised the anthropic principle argument into the argument that I can already use my own existence as an individual as tremendous evidence for that same loosening of personal identity—so that there was no improbable coincidence for me in emerging from my own begetting and the ever-so-long line of prior begettings of each of all my ancestors, supposedly also required for my existence. Whichever sperm cell of the 200,000,000 or so had made it to the egg in each of all those begettings, my existence would have been the result.

I thought lots about probability after discovering this way of applying it to both physics and metaphysics. I discovered that probability inferences were perspectival. An improbable coincidence from the perspective of the winner of a lottery would be not at all improbable for an unattached observer of the lottery. I realised that when large numbers were involved unknown prior probabilities were no problem because it would be so improbable that they had not favoured the hypothesis favourable to the evidence. I saw that one could solve the problem of induction and answer classic scepticism with this same sort of reasoning.

Along the way I developed analogies. And this was important for Sleeping Beauty. There is a hotel with countless rooms, in each an induced sleeper. In the 'easy game' all sleepers will be awakened. In the hard game only a random one will be awakened. If you are a player and find yourself awake, you can infer that it is overwhelmingly improbable from your perspective that the hard game was played, because, for you to have your evidence—that you are awake—within that hard game hypothesis, an overwhelmingly improbable coincidence for you would have had to have occurred. (For an uninvolved observer simply presented with you as a winner there would have been no improbability if the hard game was played. Such an observer could not make that inference to the easy game.)

And I thought about a player who would be awakened one or many times—but hypnotised in between any awakenings to forget them. Could the player infer during an awakening that there were many awakenings instead of only one to make it more probable that now there would have been this awakening? (I discussed this temporal case in the 'One Self' draft sent to Stalnaker, but I had been thinking about it since 1979 and I lectured about it in the early 1980s.)

Next, in the fifth part of this book, I discuss my metaphysical solution to the Sleeping Beauty problem.

Part V:
Time, Self and Sleeping Beauty

I take a different angle in arriving at the radical view. The conditions for an experience being this one are discovered by way of analysing and solving the Sleeping Beauty problem.

1. THE UNNOTICED

It took me decades to notice a bit of wordplay in the Rodgers and Hammerstein song 'Do-Re-Mi', despite having heard it a good number of times. The lyrics of the song take us through the notes of the major scale but replacing the name of every note (except for la) with a like-sounding word. We start with 'doe, a deer', climb our way up to 'sew, a needle pulling thread', and eventually reach 'tea, a drink with jam and bread; that will bring us back to do'.

Fine, but just how does tea, a drink with jam and bread, manage to bring us back to do? Is it merely, as I once thought, that after the note ti the next note that we sing is the do above it? No, there is something more substantive here. There is the dough from which the bread is made—'bread that will bring us back to do'. What is supposed to return us to do, then, is yet another homonym. As I've said, noticing this took me decades. And among the fair number with whom I've discussed the matter, nobody else had noticed it.

Let me next raise this question: Could something of much greater importance be going generally unnoticed even in what we frequently experience?

In this discussion I shall call attention to what must be the most extreme case possible of such a thing—something all-pervasive in our experience that couldn't be less generally noticed and yet couldn't be more important.

A good place to catch a first glimpse of it is in the Sleeping Beauty problem.

2. THE ORIGIN OF THE SLEEPING BEAUTY PROBLEM

In the year 2000 the philosophy journal *Analysis* published a short paper by Adam Elga called 'Self-locating Belief and the Sleeping Beauty Problem'. Since then that problem has caused a great deal of excitement.

Finding Myself: Beyond the False Boundaries of Personal Identity
Special Supplement, *Midwest Studies in Philosophy*
https://doi.org/10.5840/msp202549Supplement8

Elga in a footnote said that Robert Stalnaker, who named the problem, 'first learned of examples of this kind in unpublished work by Arnold Zuboff'. I can add here that that work, which Stalnaker saw in 1986, eventually *was* published, in 1990 in the journal *Inquiry*, as 'One Self: The Logic of Experience'.

And we must look back to this origin of the problem to find its solution. For the solution requires not just attention to points about probability, as is usual in the debate, but also, and much more crucially, attention to the metaphysical issues that were addressed in that 1990 paper—issues regarding experience, time and what a person is.

3. THE AWAKENING GAME

I like presenting the problem using much larger numbers than you'll find in the established discussion. That way the alternatives show much more starkly.

Imagine an 'awakening game', as we shall call it, in which, at the start, a single player is to be put to sleep by a hypnotist. The player will then be kept in this hypnotic sleep for a trillion days. Except that after the player is put to sleep a fair coin will be tossed to determine which of two procedures will be followed: Either the player will be awakened for a short period every one of the trillion days or will be awakened for a short period only once—on only one day randomly chosen among the trillion.

To this we must add that, at the end of any period of awakening, the hypnotist, before putting the player to sleep again, will wipe permanently from the player's mind the memory of having been awakened. Thus, whichever the number of awakenings, one or a trillion, each will seem like a first awakening.

Let us say that a player knows all this but is not told which of the two procedures is being followed in that game. Is there any way the player can infer whether this is a game of being awakened one time or a game of being awakened a trillion times?

4. AN INFERENCE TO A TRILLION AWAKENINGS

Imagine that you are the player and you now find yourself awake. It seems you can reason as follows: It would be a trillion times less probable that I would on this day be awake if only one day was to be chosen for an awakening instead of all trillion days. What I do find today—my evidence—that I am now awake—would therefore have been immensely improbable with only one awakening in the game. But it has to be immensely improbable that something immensely improbable is what is occurring. So, given this evidence of my today being awake, I must infer that the hypothesis that there are a trillion awakenings is immensely more probable than the hypothesis that there is only one.

On the incredibly rare day of awakening in a one-awakening game, such an inference would have misled you into preferring the hypothesis of a trillion awakenings, which would then have been false. But if this game had only one awakening it would also have been overwhelmingly more probable that today you would have been sleeping and therefore in no condition to engage in a misleading inference. That the inference is not misleading is thus overwhelmingly more probable than that it is.

5. THE PROBLEM

The Sleeping Beauty problem is seen from the angle of the player just before the start of the game. It seems certain that before the start of the game—before the coin determining the number of awakenings has even been tossed—you can say nothing about whether in the coming game you'll be awakened either once or a trillion times. Yet you can know then that in your very next episode of thought you will be rightly inferring that a trillion awakenings are occurring.

It is as though you are in a room where you will soon be opening a door into the next room. You know already what you will see when you open it, and what you will rightly infer on the basis of seeing that; but somehow you cannot yet make the inference. It seems that, similarly, before the game you both can and cannot make an inference. And this contradiction, because one is led to it down seemingly unavoidable paths of reasoning, is a paradox.

Those I've talked to who have had trouble seeing the problem have found they could feel the power of the paradox after I explained how the awakening game can go piggyback on an uncontroversial probability inference. And examining that inference, as we'll do after the limbering up exercise of the next section, can assist us in understanding much better the probability involved.

So, my advice is to persevere beyond this point even if you find that you cannot yet see the promised paradox. For I think that you can still have a real hope of seeing this strange and beautiful bird.

And please don't worry, if you were so inclined, that my discussion of probability will become very technical. I am allergic to equations.

6. A LIMBERING UP EXERCISE

Solving the Sleeping Beauty problem will require a clearer look at something so close that it is hard to see—one's own present moment of consciousness.

Our minds are stuck in a fuzzy view of this. So, we need a new suppleness of understanding that I hope can be acquired through some mental limbering up.

This can be through considering a stage in my old paper 'The Story of a Brain', first published in *The Mind's I*, a popular anthology of philosophical papers about the mind.

As the story begins, the friends of a young man whose body has been wholly devastated by disease are keeping his disembodied brain alive in a nutrient bath and, by using electrodes, artificially sending into his brain the same patterns of stimulation that it would have been receiving naturally if it had been in their friend's body in varieties of circumstances that were all extremely pleasant [Figure 1]. They are confident that in this way they are causing their friend to have wonderful experiences, perfectly indistinguishable for him from ones he might have been having naturally.

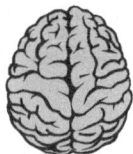

Figure 1

An accidental cutting in two of the brain gives the man's friends an idea. They will have more space in which to work if they put each hemisphere of the brain into its own nutrient bath in its own laboratory. But if the hemispheres aren't stuck together, how will the activities of each integrate with those of the other, as they would do in the production of natural experience? No problem. First wires and later radio transceivers are fitted onto the neurons on either side of the cut between the hemispheres that will transmit and receive all the impulses that the hemispheres would have been sending into each other in natural fashion if they were together [Figure 2]. (I've smoothed out some details of the story.)

Figure 2

The friends reason that the new gap in the objective circumstances of the experience, the distance between the hemispheres, could have no impact at all on its subjective character, on what it feels like to the young man. So, if, for example, the young man's experience is to be of standing in a field with the beauties of spring all around him, this would seem, in the usual way, to be centred on a head that was intact.

This distinction between the objective circumstances and the subjective character of an experience will be crucial to what we need to see. It is an easy mistake merely to merge together the objective and the subjective determinations of an experience, to think that to be intact just is to feel intact and to feel intact just is to be intact. The two do normally go together, but they are actually quite distinct. Nothing is felt if it has not been properly registered in the processing of experience, even the objective character of the processing itself. And whatever is so registered, whether truly or falsely, *will* be felt despite any failure of that feeling as a reflection of the objective character of that processing.

Next comes the part of our mental limbering up most specifically helpful for solving the Sleeping Beauty problem. We come to the distinction between the objective and subjective *time* of an experience.

The young man's friends have moved the hemispheres to labs far apart and are worried about a confusion of the pattern of interaction due to the resulting small time lags in the broadcastings of the transceivers. They overcome that problem by replacing the radio transceivers with pre-programmed 'impulse cartridges'. Let me explain.

We shall say that these friendly inducers of the young man's experience have complete knowledge beforehand of the pattern of radio transmission that each hemisphere would be receiving from the other during the course of any particular experience. A pre-programmed impulse cartridge carefully fitted onto a hemisphere's cut, where the transceivers would have been feeding into it all the impulses coming from the other hemisphere, could produce exactly the same pattern of impulses into the one to which it was fitted with no actual interaction occurring between the hemispheres (and no confusion of the pattern due to time lags in broadcasting) [Figure 3].

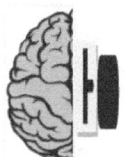 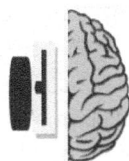

Figure 3

The friends reason as follows: How could this purely external change in objective circumstances, from radio transmission to pre-programmed cartridges, have made any difference to how the experience feels? After all, nothing could register as the least bit different within the actual workings of the hemispheres. Surely each hemisphere would still support an experience; and surely the sum of both, with their wholly continued complementing of each other, will be subjectively the same knitted-together experience that would have been had in the usual case.

What will especially interest us in this latest development, this cartridge replacement, is that simultaneity and synchronisation of the activity of the hemispheres would no longer be needed in the production of a single experience involving both hemispheres.

And so, it is now possible to have one hemisphere make its contribution to the experience on one day [Figure 4] and the other hemisphere make its contribution a day later [Figure 5] without any change at all to the feeling in the experience. The experience would not only remain subjectively centred on an intact head but would be subjectively occurring at a single time.

Monday

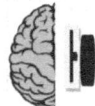

Figure 4

Tuesday

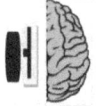

Figure 5

The young man would still feel buffeted by the cool dawn breeze, listen to the birdsong on every side, take in the sight and the fragrance of the flowers all around him and extending as far as he could see—their wild colours muted in the light and shadows of the huge rising sun. He looks down at his beautiful timepiece, and he sees the time.

The right hemisphere processes the left side of the field of vision and the left hemisphere the right side. But in the experience there would be no time difference between the left and the right of the scene. The young man does not experience one side of his visual field—and thus one side of the field he's standing in—as somehow coming first with the other not arriving till the next day. For him the whole of the field is simply there now. Using the right hemisphere, in which music appreciation is localised, he admires the birdsong's melody; and, at subjectively the same time, he's thinking of the names of the birds using the verbal skills of the left hemisphere. For him there's no day-long wait. No time difference has been registered in either of the hemispheres, and so no time difference can be experienced.

Think of how impervious this experience is to changes in its objective realisation. It would have been the same experience no matter how much time passed before the second hemisphere made its contribution. If this had been not the next day but billions of years later, it would have been impossible for this great difference in its realisation to be registering as any sort of subjective difference within the experience itself.

It would have been the same experience no matter which hemisphere was used on the first day and which on the second. And, of course, it would have been the same experience if both hemispheres had happened to be used at the same time no matter whether this was on the first day or on the second—or on any other day at all. So, on any day out of a trillion, for example, it would still have been the very same experience.

And this last is obviously a thought that has great relevance for the Sleeping Beauty problem. The inference at the heart of the problem depends on a supposed distinctness of experiences of awakening depending for their identities on the merely objective distinctness of the days out of a trillion on which the experiences would be occurring. The player within an experience of awakening crucially judges that this experience now being had would not have existed if there had been no awakening on this particular day. Such an experience on any other day would have been another one—not this one. And that is what would make all trillion days of awakening rather than only one more probable from that perspective. And yet, when thinking before the game about the single day of awakening if there is to be only one, the player is apt to think of that experience as being the same one no matter which day of the trillion it might happen to fall on.

Getting to the bottom of the Sleeping Beauty problem requires seeing that there is a conflict between these two ways of individuating an experience—objective individuation, in which the identity of the experience depends on the objective time in which it occurs, and subjective individuation, in which it does not. Our limbering up should have prepared us for seeing this conflict.

But we must also think clearly, as few people do, about probability. That, after a reminder of the problem, will be our next focus.

7. BACK TO SLEEPING BEAUTY

Recall the awakening game: A hypnotist makes a player sleep through a trillion days, except that the player will be awakened either only once, on a randomly chosen day, or else once a day on every day of the trillion. The toss of a coin determines which. And the hypnotist will, before inducing sleep again at the end of the period of any awakening, wipe from the player's mind all memory of having been awakened.

If you found yourself awake in the game, it seems you should infer that the game is one with a trillion awakenings. Otherwise your now being awake would have been extremely improbable—and it must be improbable that something improbable is what is occurring.

And recall the Sleeping Beauty problem: Just before the game starts (before the coin is even tossed) you, the player, could not infer how many awakenings there were going to be. But at that time just before the game you also could know that in your very next episode of thought you would be rightly inferring that the game contained a trillion awakenings rather than only one. So it seems that before the game you both should and should not be joining in this inference.

It is as if you already knew both what you would see when you opened a door to another room and what you would rightly conclude based on seeing it but somehow you could not yet arrive at that conclusion.

8. A STANDARD CASE

In textbooks on statistics, though there may be no examples with awakenings in them, I believe that we can often find examples using urns.

Imagine two enormous urns, each containing a trillion beads. In one urn all trillion beads are blue, whereas in the other urn only one bead of its trillion is blue. This second urn has been well stirred so that the single blue bead has nestled into a random location among the other beads.

First, let us say, a toss of a fair coin decides which of the two urns is pushed forward for sampling. Then a single bead that is randomly drawn from that urn is shown to an observer who has no other basis for judging what it contains and who understands all the circumstances I have described.

If the bead that is shown is blue, the observer should infer that it is a trillion times more probable that the urn being sampled is the urn with beads that were all of them blue. If it were instead the urn with only one blue bead, then this random drawing of a bead that was blue would have had to be something overwhelmingly improbable. But it is overwhelmingly improbable that something overwhelmingly improbable is what has occurred. Hence that hypothesis, combined with this evidence, is itself overwhelmingly improbable and we must infer that the other hypothesis, of the urn being that with all blue beads, is overwhelmingly more probable to be true. We should expect this inference to give us the wrong answer in something like once in every trillion times this is tried. But it is overwhelmingly improbable that this is such a time. And even then it would surely have been the rational inference to make.

(The fundamental principle of all empirical reasoning, as I have argued in Part II of this book, is the necessary truth that it is always most probable that the most probable thing will occur—or has occurred. What I say above, that 'it is overwhelmingly improbable that something overwhelmingly improbable is what has occurred', is simply an expression of this principle.

Let me briefly note here, with more discussion later, that it is the very same principle that also governs cases that are unlike this one in that in them it is most probable, given *all* the evidence, that an improbable event has occurred, either 1) because other evidence would have to be interpreted as even more improbable than the improbable event in question if that event had not occurred or 2) because the observation of that *locally* improbable event is had from a broad perspective that includes enough chances for such an event to occur to have rendered an occurrence probable.)

9. THE BEAD GAME

In a variation on the standard case I described in the previous section, the urn pushed forward will have each of its beads in random fashion assigned to each one of the trillion days. A single player will be awakened every day from a hypnotic sleep to view just the bead that was assigned to that day. And the player will be hypnotised each time into forgetting the awakening and what has been seen within that session. So, this is like the awakening game but with seeing a blue bead instead of simply being awakened and seeing a non-blue bead instead of remaining asleep a whole day.

Now imagine yourself to be this player having been awakened and seeing a blue bead. Surely you should infer that it is a trillion times more probable that the urn is one with a trillion blue beads. For if it were rather the urn with only one blue bead it would have been one short of a trillion times more probable that on any random day, such as this one now, you would be seeing a non-blue bead.

Note that if the urn with only one blue bead had been used then in one observation of the trillion you would have been seeing that urn's single blue bead. And then your inference to a trillion blue beads would have misled you as to the actual number of blue beads in the urn. But it must be overwhelmingly improbable that this observation of a blue bead you are now making actually is a one in a trillion fluke and therefore overwhelmingly improbable that this inference actually *does* mislead you. Furthermore, the inference to a trillion blue beads would have been the only rational inference to make even then.

10. NO PROBLEM

It is important to notice that there seems to be no Sleeping Beauty problem in the case of the bead game, despite its similarity to the awakening game. The player before the game has no reason to favour either hypothesis but in this case unproblematically knows that in the next episode of thought *either* a blue bead *or* a non-blue bead will be seen and that this will then put the player into a position to make the appropriate judgment.

(I shall not yet discuss pragmatic betting strategies. How it makes sense to bet based on an observation can, we shall eventually see, be a question that is to a large extent independent of the question of the evidential force of the observation.)

11. RELEVANT CONTENT

Let me make some points about the evidential force—and lack of it—of differing contents in the observation of a player within a bead game and variations of it.

We shall say that the player, examining a blue bead, notices a sequence of letters and digits engraved on its surface. The sequence is g3v98b6rgh0kw5. This content of the player's observation, along with the colour of the hypnotist's clothing, is surely irrelevant for the player in deciding between the urns. It has no evidential force. To have evidential force it would need to be something that would be known to be more probable in one available hypothesis than it would be in another.

But why couldn't seeing this sequence be evidence for an inference about something else, an inference in which the player proclaims the greater probability of the hypothesis that all the beads in the urn have this same precise series engraved on them? Would that not have made it more probable that this part of the content of the observation has occurred? While we are at it, why not also infer that the hypnotist always wears blue? But these proposed inferences are obviously fishy. Thoughts like these can blow our thinking way off course. Yet what could be wrong with such reasoning?

Imagine that the player has actually been provided by the organizers of the game with a choice between such a hypothesis and a rival. The player knows that if the pure blue bead urn has been selected for use in the game by coin toss then a second coin toss would determine whether either the 'uniform' or the 'randomized' blue bead urn would be used.

The beads in the uniform urn all have exactly the same sequence engraved on them, while those in the randomized urn have been engraved with sequences that were randomly determined for each bead independently from all the others. Well, would the uniform urn hypothesis not have made the occurrence of g3v98b6rgh0kw5 much more probable, since all the beads would have this same sequence on them? And so could the player not infer that it was much more probable that the uniform urn was the one that was used, in an inference much like our inference to the urn with the trillion blue beads?

The answer is no. It is no more probable that g3v98b6rgh0kw5 was the sequence selected for a uniform urn than that it was the one that happened to be engraved on a bead drawn from the randomized urn. What is fooling us is a temptation to specify *ad hoc* that the uniform urn is filled with the particular sequence that happens to have been observed. But no such specification has been offered us in the case as described. So, the observation of g3v98b6rgh0kw5 is irrelevant to and has no evidential force for deciding between these hypotheses of uniform or randomized urn. In fact, there is absolutely no reason to favour one over the other.

If, however, the player had actually been told independently of the selection of the bead that the uniform urn contained specifically only the sequence g3v98b6rgh0kw5, then this single observation of that sequence would be enormously powerful evidence for the uniform urn being the one in use. For if that sequence had instead been drawn by chance from the randomized urn, then there would have to have been an utterly improbable coincidence between the observed sequence and what had been *independently designated* as the uniform sequence in one of the only two hypotheses on offer.

The key to all such inferences is this independent designation, as opposed to a worthless ad hoc specification. Nothing that occurs is improbable unless its occurrence would be such a coincidence—between that occurrence and an independent designation of it.

For example, if we call out a sequence of 14 letters and digits at random and then check it against the random sequence on a bead, there is a probability of only 1 in 36 to the 14th power that these independently designated sequences, the sequence called out and the sequence that happens to be on the bead, will be the same. But the mere calling out of a sequence or the mere reading of a sequence as discovered on a bead involves no coincidence—and therefore no improbability—at all.

By the way, another legitimizing form of independent designation could be repetition across observations. We go back to the case where it is either a randomized urn or a uniform urn with its sequence left unspecified. Imagine that we were allowed an observation of two beads randomly drawn from the urn, instead of just one. If both beads displayed the same sequence of numbers and letters, though it would strictly be possible that this was a chance match between two sequences in the randomized urn, this evidence, the repeated sequence, would make it overwhelmingly probable for us that the urn was rather the uniform one. The matching of two individually randomized sequences, each drawn independently from the other out of the randomized urn, would be an intolerably large coincidence. Only the uniform urn hypothesis is free of this improbability.

I'll just mention that here we can see the justification for induction based on repetition for which Hume was looking. Hume put enormous stress on the role of repetition in forming our beliefs; but, as we can see, repetition is only a special case of independent designation.

12. MORE ABOUT IMPROBABILITY

I am going to leave the urns and blue beads briefly to look at a deck of cards, an example that is particularly well suited to illustrate in finer detail the important point I make above that there is no improbability without coincidence. And to this I shall add that there is no coincidence apart from a particular perspective. Thus, all probability and all probability inferences turn out to be perspectival.

The event of picking a card from a deck has a multiplicity of descriptions that could be assigned truly to it, with some of these descriptions carrying conflicting probabilities. The event of randomly selecting the deuce of spades, for example, is at once

1. 'selecting the deuce of spades', with a probability of 1 in 52,

2. 'selecting a deuce', with the probability of 1 in 13,

3. 'selecting a spade', with the probability of 1 in 4,

4. 'not selecting the queen of hearts', with the probability of 51 in 52,

5. simply 'selecting a card in the deck', whose probability, within what was given in the case, was one.

(Note that it is not merely the event that carries multiple descriptions and therein multiple probabilities. Each description implies in itself multiple descriptions and therein the multiple probabilities. For example, the description of a card as '*a* spade' requires that it also be only one particular card of the fifty-two, that it belong to only that one particular suit, that it not be the queen of hearts and so on. So, each different probability would actually attach to no more than a single aspect of a description. Each verbal description, however, can be viewed as successfully highlighting just one such aspect— the aspect that it specifically mentions. Only from within a perspective, as we'll see, can such a highlighted aspect be made salient in a judgment of probability.)

The description, along with its associated probability, that comes into play (and that, as we'll see, could be used to make inferences if appropriate rival hypotheses are available) must depend on whether from some perspective this event would involve a coincidence (and thus an independent designation).

If the deuce of spades was merely randomly drawn from a deck, the salient description of the event for everyone (apart from the card itself, were it conscious, from whose perspective this would be an improbable coincidence) would be that of merely 'selecting a card'—which involves no improbability.

But if everyone in a large group had individually made a prediction and I had happened to predict the deuce of spades while the others' predictions together pretty well covered the whole deck, for me the description of this event as 'the selection of' in particular 'the deuce of spades' would have become salient, coming along with the merely 1 in 52 probability of my random prediction coinciding with that randomly selected card.

(Notice that for me this event would not have involved two improbabilities—a supposed merely 1 in 52 probability that it may be wrongly thought everyone else shared simply in its being the deuce of spades plus, but only for me, a second 1 in 52 improbability of the coincidence with my prediction. The overall improbability of the event for me would not have been 1 in 52 *times* 1 in 52. There would be only the 1 in 52 probability of the coincidence. There would be no further improbability. Let me add that the exclamation 'How improbable!' would be appropriate for me to make when the card I predicted was drawn from the deck; but if all that has happened is my seeing that a card has been drawn, then my exclaiming 'How improbable!' would be absurd.)

But for someone else who had predicted the queen of hearts, which wasn't selected, the salient description of the event would have been 'the selection of a card other than the queen of hearts', with its high probability of 51 in 52.

If only suits were being predicted, then the salient description for a successful predictor would have been 'the selection of a spade' and the event for that predictor would have had the probability of 1 in 4.

If only one prediction (again, we'll say, of an individual card) had been made aloud in the whole group, then a match between that prediction and the card would have been a proper coincidence for the whole group, and improbable for them.

But not for someone who was viewing a large number of groups whose single predictions together covered most of the cards in the deck. The probability of a successful prediction from that perspective is the sum of all the probabilities of success for the groups included within that view so that the event for that more inclusive observer is not similarly improbable. One might say that for this observer the local improbability has been 'relaxed', while it remains a 'strained improbability' for the members of the group in which the successful prediction had occurred.

The same point could be made about a lottery with many entrants and only one winner. The description of the event as 'someone's winning the lottery' is all that is salient for the uninvolved observer; and it carries with it no improbability. But for the winner (as for the selected card were it conscious) and for anyone appropriately connected with the winner (including anyone who had predicted just that winner), the particularity of the winner becomes part of the salient description of the event, and the event must bear the low probability of one divided by the number of entrants. (And the exclamation 'How improbable!' would be appropriate enough for the lottery winner or those already close to that winner to make; but from the mouth of an uninvolved observer hearing merely that some stranger has won 'How improbable' would be absurd.)

When we say the probability of drawing a deuce of spades is 1 in 52 or the probability of winning a certain lottery is one in a million, what we are doing implicitly is thinking of the card or an entrant as designated independently of being selected and then rightly thinking that a match of just that card or entrant with the one that is randomly selected would have that degree of improbability. In the case of the lottery entrant we can easily think of the winning from the winner's angle, from which there is indeed an improbable match. Those thoughts thus spelled out make perfect sense. But, as often happens, if we then try to think clearly about the thinking itself we can easily get confused. We may easily just think that the improbability from the angle of a match belongs to that matched event itself even without the match.

The ascription to something of improbability is like the ascription to something of dangerousness. There is a way in which everyone in every situation could properly say that a tiger is dangerous. But it is also importantly true that for you, unless you are close to a tiger (perhaps having fallen into the enclosure), it actually isn't dangerous at all. In fact, the first, the unconditional attribution of dangerousness to a tiger can be nothing but shorthand for the tiger's being a danger to those it is close enough to hurt. And this has great practical implications. No action is required to save those not threatened by the tiger. And just so, we do not look for inferences to relieve an alleged 'improbability' of merely drawing an ace of spades from a deck. No, the improbability that could drive inferences would exist only for those who were in some sense 'close' to the card—for whom, that is, there was a coincidence in that card's selection (as there would be, again, for the card itself always but also for someone predicting it). So, I would not *simply* describe the result of picking a card from a deck as 'improbable'. And such 'improbability', should one still wish to ascribe it, would have to be inferentially inert for all those not especially connected to the event. It could have no force to drive an inference.

A failure to understand these points will, of course, badly distort one's view of what probability inferences consist in. Some probability theorists who do not understand this built-in perspectival character of objective probability—that is, of the mathematical probability of chances, based purely on the number of ways that events can develop—feel forced to abandon an objective account and instead to shape their understanding of probability inference around the shifting credences (degrees of belief) of those who are making the inferences.

For in the thinking of such theorists every selection of a card from a deck that is innocent of coincidence nevertheless objectively possesses only the low probability of 1 in 52. And yet, they see, we have not the slightest problem in believing that such a selection has occurred. So it must be, they think, that *following* an objectively improbable event like that one, what we do is to adjust our credences and then ascribe to the event a merely subjective probability of one, of certainty, in any further reckoning we may do. (What *I* think, of course, is that a selection of a card free of coincidence has an *objective* probability of one before, during and after it.)

It is as though an objective reckoning of the dangerousness of tigers had been abandoned—because it was thought that the description of a tiger as dangerous simply always applied—and so instead there could be nothing but a charting of the pattern of degrees of fear that tigers aroused. A subjectivist account of our fear of tigers. If a tiger is equally dangerous from every perspective, then we can only describe and never explain or justify the differing reactions of someone who has just fallen into the tiger's enclosure and someone at home reading in bed about tigers. Why should it be that one of these and not the other feels tremendous fear along with a need to brace for a tiger's attack? Well, all we can say is that these differing sorts of reactions to tigers are typical of people in situations like those. They are subjective reactions that cannot be justified by objective differences in how much danger a tiger is posing, since, these subjectivists about tigers are claiming, a tiger is always dangerous.

And such probability theorists must also be inclined to say that if we were to attempt to understand our probability inferences as simply based on the principle that what is objectively improbable is objectively improbable we should have to find ourselves repeatedly engaged in wild and futile inferences to try to push away an ever surrounding flood of objective improbability. So, as I've described, instead of understanding our beliefs as objectively justified responses to facts, they merely chart the developing pattern of the beliefs, the credences, themselves without any proper explanation of them.

(There's yet another bad reason for adopting a subjective approach to probability. We'll be discussing that in a later section on prior probabilities.)

13. RANDOM AND DIRECTED OBSERVATION

Let's return now to thinking about urns and blue beads and to thinking about the basic bead game, without the frills of engraved sequences. But let us add that a camera has recorded each of the player's observations. After the game an external observer, who could be either the player or someone else, will be shown the recording of only one day's awakening. Which day will be shown is decided in a wholly random fashion. Well, if the film watcher sees a blue bead being observed in the game, that external observer is entitled to infer that the urn of a trillion blue beads was used. Otherwise that result would have been extremely improbable. This, then, is a 'random external observation'; and it seems to provide evidence for that external observer that is every bit as good as the evidence possessed by the player this observer is watching in the film.

But in another procedure the external observer is guaranteed to see the player observing a blue bead no matter how many such observations have been made in the game (and knows of this guarantee). If there was only one blue bead observation in the trillion recordings, it would be that recording that would be shown. If there were a trillion blue bead observations, this external observer would be shown just one of these. So, under both hypotheses—with either urn being used—the same kind of thing would be seen in all relevant respects. This will be a 'directed' or 'guaranteed' external observation.

The interesting thing here is that though such a directed observer can see the player in the act of inferring that the trillion blue bead urn was used on the basis of now observing the blue bead, and though this external observer both shares the observation and agrees with the rightness of the player's making that inference on the basis of it, the external observer cannot indulge in the inference. For the player's observation is viewed by this external observer under a condition that removes its randomness relative to viewing a blue bead, since that is guaranteed either way, and there cannot for such an observer be any difference between the hypotheses in terms of which one would make that observation more probable. Hence there is a perhaps surprising perspectival character to this probability judgment. The effect is the same as that we noted in the section before this, when the winner of a lottery rightly views that win as improbable while anyone not especially connected to the winner can find no improbability at all merely in *someone* winning, which is something that was bound to happen.

This perspectival element in the inference may seem to give us a diagnosis of the Sleeping Beauty problem. Is not the player before the game facing the future inference at least somewhat like the directed, guaranteed external observer watching the recording? The pre-game player can foresee the later appropriateness of the inference but cannot at that time make the inference. But there is still a vital factor missing. The perspectival character of the inference is surprising, but it is not paradoxical; it is not contradictory. No, there is something much bigger than this lurking in our problem that needs more uncovering before we can look it in the face.

14. THE *AWAKENING* BEAD GAME

We can very easily combine the bead game with the awakening game. The same urns are used, and with one exception the same conditions obtain. Here is the change: If a non-blue bead has been assigned to a day, the player is to be left sleeping that day instead of being awakened to see it.

Imagine you are the player now awakened and seeing a blue bead. Must you not infer both that the urn that was used was full of blue beads and that you are being awakened every day to see one? For if the urn that was used had only one blue bead in a trillion, it would have been immensely more probable that you would today be sleeping and not seeing a blue bead.

Of course, if this were still the bead game the last sentence would have read 'immensely more probable that you would today be seeing a non-blue bead'. But could this one difference between the games—in what would be happening if a blue bead had *not* been assigned to a day—affect what you should be thinking when, as now, one *has* been assigned? Does it not seem that which of the two—sleeping or seeing a non-blue bead—it might have been *outside* this awakening is irrelevant? What happens, as now, when a blue bead *has been* assigned is exactly the same in either game: You simply find that you have been awakened to see it. Does it not seem, then, that you would be equally entitled in either game, if this has happened, to infer that the urn was full of blue beads and that you are being awakened to see one every one of the trillion days?

15. THE PROBLEM RETURNS

Before the awakening bead game begins the player cannot say which urn the coin toss will select, though the player can know that in the very next episode of experience that player will be rightly inferring that the urn was full of blue beads and there are a trillion awakenings in which the player is seeing them.

The Sleeping Beauty problem has returned—in the midst of what otherwise seems a standard, unproblematic case. This, I'd say, is the high-water mark of the paradox. Let us next seek its solution.

16. THE CRUCIAL DIFFERENCE BETWEEN THE GAMES

What gave the *awakening* bead game a problem that the earlier bead game did not have? Pretty obviously the crucial difference between the games is that in the awakening bead game the only actual observations are all going to be of blue beads. There will no longer be any non-blue bead experience—in place of this there will only ever be the absence of experience.

It is because there is thus no difference in the content of an awakening experience whichever urn is used that the player can be assured before the game what the content of the very next experience will be. But, then, how can that content, a blue bead, since it is the same for either urn, still count as in the least bit relevant to the inference? Something else must have taken on this role.

17. THE IMPORTANCE OF AN EXPERIENCE BEING THIS ONE

In the awakening bead game, as in the plain awakening game, any evidential force must belong entirely to the particularity of the experience in which the inference occurs, to its being *this* one; and none of the evidential force can belong to its content. The thought behind the inference must be that if the urn contained only one blue bead—and there was therefore only one awakening in all the days of the potential trillion—then it would have been extremely improbable that *this* particular awakening would have been occurring, though, again, the character, the content, of the experience could be in no relevant way different from what it would have been if the other urn had been used.

But, you might think, since I would have been guaranteed eventually to observe the lone awakening—and nothing but that awakening—in a game of only one, that would not have been a random sample among the days but rather an observation directed only to the day when an awakening occurred. And since such a game itself has a good fifty percent chance of occurring, why should it be so very improbable for this awakening just to be that one I would be guaranteed to be observing in such a game?

The answer is that what we said about a particular awakening applies just as well to a particular observation. What, after all, is that observation apart from the awakening in which it occurs? And the particular observation of an awakening, along with the awakening itself, could only have occurred on the one day to which it belonged. Thus, the lone observation in a one-awakening game would not have been this observation but another if, as was overwhelmingly more probable, not this day but another had been selected for an awakening.

So, we see that this particular observation of awakening—the only observation that you now possess—was not at all guaranteed to occur in such a game. On the contrary: The occurrence of this observation in a one-awakening game would have been a trillion times less probable than its occurrence in a game with a trillion awakenings.

But was it really? So far, I have only been explaining and defending one view of this question, a view that can easily seem to be the only one possible. It will help us in opening our minds to the alternative if we give a name to the focus of the difference.

We have seen that in this inference there is no relevant content. All that is relevant for the inference is what the scholastics called 'haecceity' (hek see ity), the 'thisness' of a thing, as contrasted with its 'quiddity', its 'whatness'. And the thing whose haecceity must be used as the evidence for this inference is experience, consciousness itself. But can the experience being *this* one really *be* proper evidence? That turns out to be a metaphysical question.

18. RIVAL METAPHYSICAL VIEWS

There are two ways to think about the identity of a particular experience. One way allows the particularity of an awakening in the game to be proper evidence and the other does not. I shall be arguing that an ambiguity in our thinking between these views is responsible for the Sleeping Beauty paradox. I'll then show that the reasoning of the game can settle which metaphysical view is right and that the same reasoning applied in a many players version of the game can settle the all-important issue of personal identity.

19. OBJECTIVE (OR STRICT) INDIVIDUATION

It is undeniable that any experience feels like uniquely 'this' one to its experiencer at the time of having the experience. The feeling of being 'this' is a basic, thoroughly pervasive feature of the subjective character of every experience. It consists, I would say, in nothing but the immediacy with which the content of that experience is felt. 'This' pain is right here in my awareness (which is what makes it so unpleasant). That other pain, in another experience, however, is not in that way immediate from the perspective of this experience.

According to what I shall call the 'objective individuation' of experience, however, that an experience actually *is* this experience rather than another depends not only on the feeling within it of being 'this' (without which it would not even *be* an experience) but also on further factors that are purely objective—the factors of whose it is and when it occurs. An experience that was someone else's or that was mine but at another time could not have been this particular one.

In the games we have so far been considering, one of these factors, the *possessor* of an awakening experience, is always the same—it is the one player. So what would for our needs distinguish the experiences we are considering, and thus establish for each its unique haecceity, would be only the objective factor of the *time* at which the experience was occurring.

When in our thinking about the game we are contemplating the trillion awakenings version, we are naturally compelled to think in this strict way about what is required for an experience to be this one rather than another. How could one day's experience be anything but distinct from all those other experiences in the trillion days? And what can be making that experience distinct from the others except for the difference in their times of occurrence?

(We could expect that, as it happens, there will also be at least small differences in the *content* of the different experiences, but that cannot be what determines their haecceities. The existence of this experience cannot depend on any or all of the countless details in it that could so easily have worked out differently. The content might have been totally different in character and it still have been this experience in the only sense that interests us. I hope it is obvious that we are not talking about 'this experience' in the sense we would if we were speaking of 'the experience of flying' or 'the experience of being in the awakening game'.)

If we next apply this strict style of thinking to our consideration of the single-awakening version of the game, we must find that the existence of any particular experience of awakening will be immensely improbable. For it would be overwhelmingly more probable that any experience of the player had not existed because its existence was tied to a time that was not randomly selected for the single awakening.

Thus the player can use the existence of this current experience as evidence to infer the immensely greater probability of the trillion awakenings hypothesis that would have favoured that experience's existence by so much more. Now I hope it is clear that this evidential force of the haecceity of the experience is entirely owing to this strict, objective individuation of experience.

20. SUBJECTIVE (OR RELAXED) INDIVIDUATION

The second way of thinking about the individuation of experience is relaxed. When we are contemplating the single awakening version of the game, despite our ability also to view it as governed like the trillion awakenings by objective individuation, we are nevertheless strongly inclined to think instead of the player as being in one and the same experience of awakening no matter when it might be occurring within the trillion days.

For when we are not thinking squarely of the contrasting identities of other awakenings, the individuation by times tends to lose its hold on us. We are inclined rather to think of the single experience of awakening much more importantly from within it, in terms of what would be the remaining relevant factor in its particularity, just the subjective feeling of its being 'this' experience. That feeling of being 'this' would, of course, be precisely as strong on any of the trillion days an awakening might occur. And its time will simply be picked out from within that one awakening as 'this' time. Whichever time this experience happens to be occurring will thus have become 'this' time from within the experience. The time of the experience is no longer in the driver's seat with the feeling of its being 'this' as the passenger. It is the other way around: We allow this subjective judgment of being 'this' to govern completely the question of whether the experience in any time does indeed qualify to *be* 'this' experience. And thus it becomes extremely easy—in fact inevitable—for this very same experience of the player to have occurred even in the single-awakening version of the game.

But this relaxed style of individuation must therein rob the awakening's haecceity of all the evidential force that it had seemed to have within objective individuation. For, within subjective individuation neither hypothesis would make it any more probable than the other that this awakening would be occurring. In effect, the player, much like the earlier described directed external observer of the game through a recording, would be engaging in a guaranteed, directed observation of awakening rather than in a random one, since awakening would be guaranteed to be viewed within this same one experience whichever way the game was played. And, as we earlier saw regarding that directed external observer, this must spoil the inference.

21. A SINGLE NOW VERSUS MULTIPLE NOWS

I said that it was easy to adopt subjective individuation when considering the single awakening in our strange game. But the most natural way in which we normally regard our experience already amounts to an embracing of subjective and a rejection of objective individuation, though, of course, that commitment has not been clear to us.

We strongly tend to see ourselves as always within a single now, within a numerically singular experience of changes. The times change and the content develops, but these are doing so within a single experience that is always necessarily present. But this single now is not, as philosophers have often thought in trying to represent it, an objectively moving present time. A time cannot move; all movement is within time, not of it. All that the singularity of now involves is that the changing content of experience, whatever may be its objective time of occurrence, is equally immediate and therefore equally possessing the merely *subjective* character of happening now for the experiencer.

To think instead that any variation in time individuates a distinct now, a distinct experience, can involve us with the problem that, since times can be distinguished into smaller and smaller segments, the present and this experience must be razor thin. What could really belong to it? And, one might ask, how could a single self be somehow carried from one of these distinct experiences into another? A buddhistic, Humean falling apart of the self threatens.

The single now, as subjective individuation, would wreck the Sleeping Beauty inference. For it would dissolve away all the improbability in an experience of awakening being this one.

22. THE SOLUTION OF THE SLEEPING BEAUTY PROBLEM

The paradox depends on believing three claims, two of which are not consistent with each other. The three claims are:

1. Before the game starts I could have no way of saying that either number of awakenings is more or less probable than the other. (Both objective and subjective individuation would seem to agree with that claim.)

2. Before the game starts I can fully anticipate the particularity of the next experience—its being simply 'this one'—just as it will be discovered during the game. (Only subjective individuation can agree with that.)

3. From within any awakening I could use its particularity to infer the immensely higher probability that there are a trillion awakenings. (Only objective individuation can agree with that.)

It is from these three beliefs put together that we get the contradictory impression of before the game not being able to make the inference and yet then having hold of all that will be required to make the inference.

If we stayed consistently within subjective individuation, we would think that the player before the game could fully anticipate the particularity of the first experience of the game, whether it was the experience of the first of a trillion awakenings or else the (probably) much later experience of a sole awakening in the game. The current imagining of it would have present in it everything that will be required to make it 'this'. But that now fully available particularity could in no way serve, either in the game or now, as evidence for an inference regarding how many awakenings there would be.

If we stayed consistently within objective individuation, however, we would think that the player before the game could only be imagining what the first awakening would feel like. The player could not somehow now be grasping the later particularity that will have to depend on the objective time of its occurrence. Thus the player is not at all now in the position that will be achieved later, in any awakening of the game, of being able to use the fact that *this* experience is occurring to infer the overwhelmingly greater probability of the hypothesis that would be making its existence overwhelmingly more probable—the hypothesis of the trillion awakenings.

One might mistakenly take this perspectival nature of the inference within objective individuation to be itself the whole problem and then think to have solved it merely through recognizing that such an inference can indeed have such a nature. That is something that Elga seems to do in his paper. He says, 'Thus the Sleeping Beauty example provides a new variety of counterexample to Bas Van Fraassen's 'Reflection Principle'.[1] The Reflection Principle is one that would have required uniformity between our player's pre-game and in-game judgments.

Yet the perspectival nature of the inference, though perhaps it is surprising, is not paradoxical. A paradox occurs when natural tendencies of thought produce a contradiction. But there is no contradiction in the perspectival character of inference.

Within objective individuation the player before the inference is merely anticipating in a general way a future moment of inference whose particular haecceity is in no way available to that player at that earlier time. So, of course that player can't make the inference.

You may remember my providing an image of our paradox: It is as though you already knew both what you would see when you opened the door to another room and what you would rightly conclude based on seeing it but somehow you could not yet arrive at that conclusion. That does represent well enough what we would have if we inconsistently shifted views from subjective to objective individuation between anticipation and inference in the way I have been claiming is the source of the paradox.

But this image is not parallel with what we would have if we stayed strictly within objective individuation regarding both the inference and the anticipation of it. A suitable parallel might be rather that only your later possible presence in some one particular room among a trillion will, if it occurs, be serving you as evidence for an inference that therefore you cannot make now. There is no suggestion here of a paradox in comparing what you know now with what you will be in a position to know later.

---

1.   Adam Elga, 'Self-locating Belief and the Sleeping Beauty Problem'. *Analysis* 60: 146.

The Sleeping Beauty problem only arises, then, when we inconsistently take the player before the game to have hold of proper evidence without being able to make the inference. But only the subjective view allows the player to have hold of what would only be proper evidence in the objective view.

Here is a chart that displays the sorting out of relationships that solves the problem:

	Pre-game Inference?	Full Anticipation?	In-game Inference?
Subjective Ind	No	Yes	No
Objective Ind	No	No	Yes
Paradox	No	Yes	Yes

Which view is right, subjective or objective? I think we can quickly answer that central metaphysical question by way of a powerful probability inference.

But it would be good first to look at the issue of prior probabilities.

(Let me briefly clarify how all this applies to the standard formulation of the Sleeping Beauty problem. The version most commonly discussed—introduced by Elga in 2000—differs in scale but not in structure. Instead of a player facing either one or a trillion awakenings, the player—called 'Sleeping Beauty'—is awakened either once (on Monday) if a fair coin lands heads, or twice (on Monday and Tuesday, with memory erased between awakenings) if the coin lands tails. Beauty awakes in the game. Can she infer how the coin landed? Now I'll apply the metaphysical framework to that.

(On the view of objective individuation, being in this particular awakening is more probable if the coin landed tails—since there are then two such awakenings rather than one. The probability of heads is thus one-third rather than one-half. This is the reasoning behind the 'thirder' position.

(On the view of subjective individuation, however, the current thisness of the experience remains the same regardless of how many awakenings occur. This awakening that Beauty finds herself in has the same chance of occurring whether there is one or two. The fair coin toss is therefore the sole determinant of the probability, and that remains one-half. Demonstrating that subjective individuation is correct—as I am about to do—will show that the halfer position is right in the standard case, though for a deeper reason than halfers typically provide.)

23. PRIOR PROBABILITIES

In each of our cases a fair coin was used to decide which urn would be pushed forward or which version of the awakening game would be played. This meant that what are called the 'prior probabilities' of the competing hypotheses were equal. That is, apart from consideration of which hypothesis made the evidence more probable, it was equally probable that either was true. (Some may here notice that I am not defining prior probabilities in the usual way—in terms of the credences of those making the inference. As always, my approach to probability is objective. I hope that what I have said earlier about perspective and what I shall say in this section about how prior probabilities can be dealt with as purely objective will be seen to justify that approach.)

What should we think in a case where we don't know such objective prior probabilities? Let's try one.

In this case there are once again our familiar two urns, each with a trillion beads, all blue beads in one and only one blue bead in the other. But this time we don't know what decided which would be pushed forward for sampling. A bead is randomly selected, and it is a blue bead. Can we not still, as in our earlier uncontroversial cases, confidently say that it is overwhelmingly more probable that the urn pushed forward was that with all blue beads because if it had been the other urn something overwhelmingly improbable must just have occurred and it is overwhelmingly improbable that something overwhelmingly improbable occurred?

But some people think there is a problem with judging the probabilities of hypotheses in light of the evidence when their objective prior probabilities are unknown. They even demote such probability judgments to being merely 'subjective' or 'inductive'. I have consistently maintained that this is mistaken; but let's look at what worries them.

What if, unknown to us, the objective prior probabilities had made it overwhelmingly improbable that the urn with all blue beads was pushed forward. For example, 'for all we know' (as these worriers might say), behind the scenes it could have been that pushing forward the urn with all blue beads depended on pulling out the blue bead by chance in a single selection from the urn containing only one blue bead in a trillion. If a non-blue bead had been drawn, then that same urn with only one blue bead (and the drawn bead thrown back into it) would then have been pushed forward. So it would have been a trillion times *more* probable that the urn that was pushed forward was the one that, in turn, would have made it a trillion times *less* probable that a blue bead would be drawn in the selection that we were to witness. The two improbabilities, of the good urn being pushed forward and of the bad urn yielding a blue bead in a random selection, would in that case have precisely equaled each other so that each hypothesis would have been equally probable (or, more to the point, equally improbable) *given* the evidence of the blue bead.

But I say that we can easily infer that it was overwhelmingly improbable that the prior probabilities themselves were anything like that. Our principle that we must consider it improbable that something improbable occurred reaches back unstoppably to what is happening behind the scenes as well as in them, to what is happening, objectively, in the determination of the prior probabilities.

If the objective prior probabilities were bad for the hypothesis that is good for producing the evidence, then our evidence of the blue bead being drawn would have been condemned to be improbable *whichever* hypothesis was true—a condemnation that is itself improbable. For within such an *overall* hypothesis (including within it a theory of what the prior probabilities were), the hypothesis that *favoured* the evidence would be supposed to involve an improbability while, of course, the occurrence of the evidence within the hypothesis that did *not* favour it would have to remain improbable (however much that hypothesis may be favoured by the prior probabilities). With this wretched overall hypothesis we have to swallow an improbability whichever hypothesis is true. Well, we must then simply regard a hypothesis that the unknown objective prior probabilities made the evidence improbable as itself improbable.

A powerful source of confusion is this: There is a perfectly fine equation for figuring such probabilities, which has an unquestioned objective a priori status; but prior probabilities must be plugged into it. This is the equation given in Bayes' theorem. But what if the objective prior probabilities are not known? Then the hungry equation seems to require some feeding. And according to Bayes' postulate, unwisely, I think, tacked on to Bayes' theorem, what one should do is put equal prior probabilities for each hypothesis into the equation to represent their being equally unknown. In other words, in such cases we are being advised to calculate probability based on our subjective credences. This is surely a category mistake born of frustration. This is not as obviously bad as would be the advice to treat all the variables in algebraic equations whose values one hasn't yet discovered as being equal—in order to represent one's equal state of ignorance regarding them—but it's the same kind of muddle.

The right view of the mathematics, I think, is that weighing the hypotheses simply in terms of their favourability to the evidence already gives you their objective probabilities when combined with that evidence. Then the objective prior probabilities would, if not directly known, be merely missing further information that one should anyway expect to favour the hypothesis that is favourable to the evidence—because otherwise something less probable would have to have been what occurred, which must be less probably the case.

(Now, where the difference in how much the hypotheses would favour the evidence is small, the unknown prior probabilities might have been decisive, and not knowing them would be important. But not so in the sort of case that we shall next be concerned with, in which there is a massive difference in how much each hypothesis would have favoured the evidence.)

This issue needed discussion because we know that the prior probabilities of the two metaphysical hypotheses were not fixed by tossing a fair coin. The prior probability of one of the hypotheses must be one—certainty—because its truth would be necessary. That of the other must be zero. In our next inference we shall be discovering the most probable overall metaphysical hypothesis, including its prior probability of one.

24. THE FIRST METAPHYSICAL INFERENCE—IN THE GAME

Let's go back to the setting of the awakening game, but this time the player is assured of being awakened only one time in the trillion days. There will be no hypothesis available of a trillion awakenings. But the player is nevertheless offered a choice between two hypotheses—two metaphysical hypotheses, objective and subjective individuation. You are the player finding yourself awake. What should you infer?

It would have been terrifically improbable that this experience existed only if objective individuation were right. It is overwhelmingly improbable that something overwhelmingly improbable is what is occurring. Hence you, the player, must accept as overwhelmingly more probable that subjective individuation is true.

If objective individuation were right there would still have been a moment *like* this, and then the inference would have been misleading. But it is overwhelmingly improbable that *this* experience would have existed to *be* that misleading inference; and hence it is overwhelmingly improbable that this inference *is* misleading.

Please note the perspectival nature of this inference. No external observer, including the player when in another experience, could possibly use the haecceity of *this* experience to make an inference against objective individuation. For from outside the experience it could only have counted as the one that happened to exist. From any such external angle an observation of it would have been directed and guaranteed. Only from within the experience would its existence have been an improbable coincidence if objective individuation were true. Thus, only from within this experience can its existence be used to establish the overwhelming probability that subjective individuation is right.

25. THE FIRST METAPHYSICAL INFERENCE—IN YOUR LIFE

Need such a metaphysical inference be confined only to a fantastic game? Not at all. Just such an inference can be made by you right now.

If objective individuation were true, then it would have been extraordinarily improbable that this experience of yours existed. For its existence, its haecceity, would have required you to be existing and conscious in just one small period of time, the time at which your experience is actually occurring. If you and your experience had instead existed at any other time, this experience would never have come to be.

Thus, the hypothesis of objective individuation would have made the evidence, this experience, an overwhelmingly improbable occurrence. The other hypothesis, subjective individuation, would have involved no such improbability at all. Well, it must be overwhelmingly improbable that something overwhelmingly improbable is what is occurring. Hence it must be overwhelmingly more probable for you from the perspective of this experience that subjective individuation is true.

26. THE RELATION OF EXPERIENCE TO TIME

Remember now our young man's experience of standing in the field at sunrise and how it seemed this must remain the same one experience even with an objective realisation that had the hemispheres of his brain making their contributions to it on objectively different days—or with an objective gap of a billion years between them. Only subjective individuation can allow this resilience of an experience. And now we've seen also that thinking otherwise is statistically incredible. Objective individuation regarding the time of an experience is at once incoherent and immensely improbable. Let's look some more at the actual relation of experience to time.

Imagine that your experience of reading this section is somehow instantaneously frozen at its mid-point and then one billion years later instantaneously thawed to continue just as it would have done without the freezing. Well, the objective billion-year gap could not register on you at all. The experience would be subjectively the same as it would have been without the gap. The content of the later half would seamlessly flow from the earlier.

Now imagine that, first, your entire experience of reading this section occurs in normal fashion. And, then, all is instantaneously frozen and somehow worked upon to restore it to precisely the condition it was in just at the beginning of the second half of the experience. And, after a billion-year gap, it is instantaneously thawed and made to continue precisely as it did, in every subjective detail, the first time.

In this case there is a precise objective repetition of the second half of the reading of this section. But what will there be subjectively? I would argue that, despite the objective repetition, there could be no subjective repetition. In the previously considered case of the billion-year gap, the first half of the experience of reading this section subjectively continued seamlessly into the second. Well, that must still happen in this repetition case—but it must happen also with the continuation that first occurred, the one without a gap. But surely there can be experienced here only one such seamlessly joined continuation.

So precise objective repetitions cannot register subjectively as multiple episodes of experience but only as one, no matter when or how many they may be.

If differences in content were to be introduced between the two continuations of the experience of reading this section, then there would indeed be subjectively more experience—where the differences came in there would be unconnected experiencing of the variant parts. But still no repetition of what was precisely the same.

If this is right, then, startlingly, in a strange choice between there being one thousand precisely repeated day-long episodes of torture and only one such episode to which, however, a stepping on one's foot was added, it would be wise to choose the thousand repetitions because they would be subjectively only the single episode but without a stepping on one's foot.

One can easily do thought experiments in which objective temporal order comes apart from the subjective order. A science fiction or magic reordering in objective time of stages of your experience of reading this section that perfectly preserved all the subjective character of the experience in each of those stages could result in no subjective difference in your experience of the reading. What would naturally have been the first stage would be experienced as first and the last as last even if objectively they came the other way around. (Line up alphabet blocks in any order you like: That will have no effect at all on the alphabetical order of the letters on them.) And all these moments would be experienced simply as 'now' whenever objectively they had been made to occur.

Objective individuation is confused—it is not only incredibly improbable but incoherent. It would have us expect that when an objective time was gone, was past, then the experience that was tied to it would be subjectively gone as well. But, as we have just seen, what does not yet exist may be subjectively earlier than what is past. And all of that is subjectively 'this time', 'now', whatever the objective time of its occurrence.

27. A PROOF THAT CONTENT DOES NOT INDIVIDUATE EXPERIENCES

Recall that the inspiration for thinking of experience in terms of subjective individuation came to us when we considered the case of a single awakening, whereas when we considered the case of a trillion awakenings we tended instead strongly to favour objective individuation. Think again of the trillion awakenings and feel once again the inspiration to distinguish experiences among them.

Well, now that we have eliminated basing such a distinction of haecceities on the objective times of experience, there might yet be a temptation to maintain such a distinction based on another condition that we had earlier dismissed as incapable of supporting it.

We had said that the particular content of experience could not play any role in defining the haecceity of experience because an experience would still have been *this* one despite any differences that might have developed in its content.

But now we are faced with a trillion packages, as we might call them, of at least slightly differing contents of experience that we realise cannot be distinguished as belonging to different experiences by any difference in the objective times in which they occur.

In one awakening, let us say, the player is facing right on the bed while being roused from sleep while in another the player is at first facing left and is therefore seeing very different things in the background. We may still be powerfully tempted to think that these contents must belong to different experiences. Hence we might be powerfully tempted to think that the details of content do somehow manage to mark off distinctions of experiences in the sense we are after.

But there is a way of showing that this hypothesis, like that of objective times doing that job, must be immensely improbable from the perspective of the experience in question.

Consider all the detail that makes up one such package of contents. Let's concentrate on the detail in the visual field. In theory a ten by ten grid could be drawn that divided the visual content of a moment of that vision into a hundred squares. And we could easily specify some ten ways in which a colour or shape in each square of visual content might have been different. The number of possible variations in visual content thus highlighted would amount to ten to the hundredth power (a googol), which is immensely greater than the number of particles in the entire visible universe.

If the player's experience would only have existed should all of its package of content have been exactly as found, the odds against the existence of this, the experience in which the inference is occurring, are immense beyond belief. If, however, subjective individuation is true and therefore it does not matter to the existence of 'this' experience what content it has—because all content must be equally 'this' merely due to its quality of immediacy—then there is no improbability in the existence of either this experience or the content that has been relieved of that responsibility for individuating it. So, the haecceity of experience is independent of the content of the experience as well as of the objective time of the experience.

28. STRATEGY

Even if the haecceity of the player's experience in the awakening game could not be a basis for that player to infer the greater probability of a trillion awakenings, there could still be a pragmatic, strategic reason for favouring that hypothesis.

Various schemes might be devised for allowing the player within the game to bet on which version is being played. There could be, for example, a certain scheme in which the player makes only one bet covering a whole trillion-day game. In this scheme, in each awakening the player is asked to vote, so to speak, for which way to bet. If the player is awakened a trillion times, a majority vote will decide how to bet. If there's only one awakening, of course, the vote during that one awakening decides it.

A player who believes in objective individuation would infer each time that the version is that of a trillion awakenings and might be imagined betting on that version simply based on that inference. But obviously that player will only have a 50% chance of winning. For that will be a winning bet when the coin decides for a trillion awakenings and a losing bet when the coin decides for only one. Perhaps it looks, then, as though the inference itself is wrong since it couldn't have helped with that betting. But, as we'll see, a good betting strategy and truth-finding cannot be so directly correlated.

Consider an alternative scheme. In this scheme a player bets once every awakening. Then, under this scheme by contrast with the other, the player has a chance of winning every one of a trillion bets in the trillion awakenings version. And if the one awakening version has been played only one bet will be lost. So, the right way to bet, as a pragmatic question, is surely to bet on the trillion awakenings whenever awakened. But is this at all connected to whether a truth-seeker would be right to infer that the trillion awakenings is being played? No.

For notice that a player who believes in subjective individuation and therefore cannot use an awakening as evidence, would *still* be wise, as a strictly pragmatic matter of strategy, to bet on the trillion awakenings version in the betting scheme just described and have a trillion wins if that version is played and only one loss if it isn't.

This is not, however, merely a crass question of trying to increase one's winnings. There is a quasi-epistemological aspect to it. Whether betting or not, a player who tends to favour the trillion awakenings could be properly aiming at increasing the amount of correctness in favouring a hypothesis. If it is the trillion awakenings version, by favouring that the player would be correct a trillion times. And if it is the single awakening, being wrong would happen only once.

29. THE MANY PLAYERS AWAKENING GAME

There were two objective factors in objective individuation. So far, we have eliminated one of these but have not touched the other, the identity of the possessor. We must next turn to the question of whether that condition is really binding on the haecceity of this experience. The reasoning will be parallel to that we have already seen. Arriving at its conclusion regarding personal identity will allow us to deepen our understanding of the conclusion concerning time.

In the many players awakening game, instead of one player with a trillion times of potential awakenings we have a trillion players, each with the possibility of awakening once, at the one time of the playing of the game. The game takes place in a colossal hotel with a trillion bedrooms. In each room is a player who has been put into a hypnotic sleep. Let's say a fair coin will be tossed (even though we've seen the unimportance of this detail) to determine which of two versions of the game will be played. In one version all trillion players are to be awakened. In the other only one player, selected at random, will be awakened. Imagine that you are a player, aware of these conditions, who has just been awakened.

It seems that you should infer that the trillion awakenings version has been played. Why?

You find yourself awake, awake in *this* experience. (Outside of an experience that *was* this, you could never have found yourself at all. For you can only ever identify yourself by picking yourself out as *this* experiencer—that is, whatever experiencer is having the experience that *is* this.) If only one player had been awakened, it would have been overwhelmingly improbable that *you* would have found yourself awake. It would have been overwhelmingly more probable that someone else would have been awakened and that *this* awakening experience had not occurred. There would have been an experience *like* this one if there had been only one awakening, but because almost certainly it wouldn't have been your experience (in other words, *this* person's experience), the haecceity of the experience almost certainly would have been different.

Now, that lone awakener would have reasoned just as you are doing and have been misled by such reasoning into thinking that all trillion players were awake. But it would have been overwhelmingly improbable that *you* would have been *that* lone awakener and that *your* inference *is* misleading.

We can think of two interestingly different styles of observation that an external observer of this game might engage in. In a random observation, the external observer would be brought to observe a randomly selected room. If what is observed there is a player awake, the external observer, like the player, can use that player as a random sample whose being awake would have been improbable if there had been only one awakening. But in a directed, guaranteed observation, which involves being brought to the room of an awakener either way, while that observed awakener is properly using the awakening as evidence for the trillion awakenings version, the guaranteed external observer, while agreeing that the awakener's reasoning was appropriate, could not use that same awakening as evidence to reach that conclusion. It would have no evidential force for that observer because an awakening would be seen whichever hypothesis was true. So, the inference is perspectival. Only a player or a *random* external observer can make the inference.

30. THE SECOND METAPHYSICAL INFERENCE—IN THE GAME

Let us now say that every player has been reliably informed before the game that for sure only one random player of the sleeping trillion will be awakened. When that one is awakened it will be nothing improbable for us from our perspective outside the game.

Imagine, however, that you are the one awakened player. Since you know for sure that there is to be only one, there is no hypothesis of all trillion awakenings to dissolve away the incredible coincidence between the supposedly demanding conditions for the existence of this, *your* experience, and a random selection of just one awakener in the trillion. It would have been overwhelmingly more probable that the single random sample you had of a player—you—would not have come to consciousness in a game with only one awakener. And you must therefore deeply suspect the assurance you've been given that there was only one player awakened of the trillion. But then you are made aware of a different sort of hypothesis that can rid you of this seemingly indigestible improbability without opposing the assurance that there has been only one player awakened.

For there are two crucially different metaphysical hypotheses available. One is the familiar though trimmed down objective individuation of experience that we've already been assuming in our description of the many players game. It is trimmed down, recall, because at this stage of our discussion it places only one condition on the haecceity of this experience—that it be had by one particular objectively distinguishable possessor of experience. And that hypothesis is the very assumption in the thinking of this player that creates the appearance of improbability that is plaguing the player.

The rival hypothesis is all-out subjective individuation, completely loosened from any objective requirements—whether of time *or* possessor—for the existence of this experience. According to this subjective individuation both the time and the possessor are merely picked out as 'this' time or 'this' person from within an experience that is itself 'this' for the reason of nothing more than the immediacy with which its contents are experienced. An aspect of this immediacy of contents is its first-person quality—its being experienced as 'mine'. Thus, just as it would have been 'this' awakening at 'this' time no matter *when* it occurred, so also would it have been 'this' awakening *of 'this' awakener*—the one picked out as 'this' within the experience—no matter which objectively distinguishable conscious organism was awakened. Any experience of awakening would be this. Any experience would be mine. Any experiencer would be me.

So, according to all-out subjective individuation my awakening would be easy, relaxed, inevitable, and wholly free of improbability with regard to either its objective time of occurrence or the objective identity of an organism experiencing it. The awakened player must embrace this hypothesis as overwhelmingly more probable to be true than the rival hypothesis.

(A word about words. According to objective individuation there are in this game a trillion distinct awakeners, distinct experiencers, distinct persons, distinct subjects of experience and self-interest, who would be having experience with a trillion distinct haecceities should all of them awaken. As we continue down that list, from awakeners to subjects of experience, the commitment in the wording becomes more and more metaphysical in the direction of objective individuation. Even so, subjective individuation could accept any of those ways of referring to the objectively distinguishable 'organisms' (if I may use a clearly neutral way of speaking) and simply add, 'But all of them would be me'. Alternatively, subjective individuation could be represented as saying, the other way around, 'You and I are the same person, the same centre of experience and so on'. It is not the language that is important in this but rather the metaphysics we are trying to express by using it.)

Is subjective individuation, then, a trillion times more probable than objective individuation? That's nowhere near a large enough number. Why? Forget remaining asleep in the game. Just think of all the organisms that according to objective individuation would have been defining distinct haecceities of experience but will never come into existence. How much greater the probability, if objective individuation is right, that our awakener's required organism had instead been one of the countless numbers left sleeping the much bigger sleep of never existing at all.

31. THE SECOND METAPHYSICAL INFERENCE—IN YOUR LIFE

Objective individuation says that your own coming to be was unbelievably improbable. Subjective individuation says that your coming to be was as easy as pie. We arrive once again at the inference to universalism that was presented in Part III.

But now we can also see this as part of an inference to full-blown subjective individuation.

Let me here add the wrinkle that an inference to universalism and to full-blown subjective individuation was already implied within the first metaphysical inference, the inference against the confinement of this experience to an objective time. For if the haver of this experience were limited to just one possessor, objectively defined as it would be in the usual view of personal identity, then that would also have required the experience to be existing during the particular objective period of time in which that subject of experience existed.

Part VI:
The Reader and the Intergalactic Philosopher: A Monologue

I take yet another angle in arriving at the radical view. A science fiction thought experiment tests whether the reader's experience is a token or a type.

Here I shall be not merely recounting but *enacting with you* a science fiction story. It is a story that embodies a series of thought experiments developed from the basic thought experiment in D. C. Dennett's well-known paper 'Where Am I?'

I must apologize beforehand—you, my kind reader, will be playing a role in this little drama that will at times require that you be treated rather roughly—at least in your imagination. But, as I hope you will eventually agree, it's all for your own good. One final word before the curtain rises. What are called simply 'the exercises' in this story will be fictional. But as thought experiments, experiments and exercises in thought, they will be fully genuine in the only way we shall need them to be. And now the play begins.

As I sit here in my study writing this I am looking at a penny on a table and asking myself, 'What distinguishes this penny from all other things?'

Perhaps it is its description, which makes it different, for example, from the table it is on, since a table has a very different description from a penny. But here, also on the table, I see another penny with an extremely similar description to that of the first. Yet I know that if I looked closely enough I could find differences, tiny scratches and so on, that do distinguish the two pennies from each other.

But what if somewhere within the whole of reality there exists some other thing that is exactly like this penny—even in all the tiniest respects? It is at least conceivable that there is such a duplicate. And if, as some cosmologists have thought, the universe is infinite, then it could seem that every occurrence in it, no matter how detailed its description might be (as long as that stops short of being infinitely complex), should be expected to pop up not only more than once but infinite times. So perhaps I haven't yet found a way

Finding Myself: Beyond the False Boundaries of Personal Identity
Special Supplement, *Midwest Studies in Philosophy*
https://doi.org/10.5840/msp202549Supplement9

of distinguishing this penny from all other things. Through these descriptions I seem only to have distinguished an extremely detailed *type* of thing, of which there could be conceivably more than one *token* [in terminology explained in Part I]. Even if there happens to be only one, it seems I have not yet succeeded in getting at what properly makes it this particular thing, distinct from all others.

Ah, but what about that part of a description that reaches out into the context? This penny, for example, is closer to my right hand than that one is. It has unique such relationships to all other things. But no matter how far out these relational descriptions reach there seems to be a conceivability remaining of even all of that being precisely duplicated. Is this complex of relations infinite in extent? I can still in some way think of there being a distinct such infinite reality that has precisely the same description. As I've already pointed out, so long as we limit ourselves to only descriptions we are talking about types of things rather than particular individuals that are the tokens of those types.

Yet it seems that I can in fact easily distinguish this penny from all other things if I do so not through its description but merely, as I've already been doing, through identifying it as 'this' one, the one I am currently attending to. It seems that by using an indexical term like 'this' or 'that' I can cut right through to the very thing itself, captured in its uniqueness simply through my reference to it. Or can even that go wrong?

First, notice how the indexical reference that thus seems capable of distinguishing a thing in such an ultimate way is rooted in the particularity of the consciousness that is doing the referring. It is in relation to that consciousness that the tokens are identified by it. The consciousness is the anchor. But confidence in this anchoring must depend on an assumption that the consciousness itself is a token. And that is what I am going to be bringing into question. But let me begin with the point that there can be 'illusions of singularity' regarding the *objects* of consciousness.

Imagine that this penny, lying on a table, is broadcast on television (as part of an especially dull programme). Well, it seems that despite its more mediated connection with me I could still be picking out this penny simply by pointing to the screen and referring to 'this penny they are broadcasting'.

But imagine next that what is actually happening, unknown to me, is that two qualitatively identical pennies, on qualitatively identical tables in different television studios, are being broadcast at the same time and at the same frequency to the television I am watching. It will still seem to me that I can succeed in distinguishing a single particular penny when I point to the screen and say 'this one'. But I'd be mistaken. We could say that I was subject here to an 'illusion of singularity'. This sort of thing could easily happen in much less contrived cases as well. For example, I might wrongly believe that I have only one penny in my pocket and talk or think about 'the penny in my pocket'. Now let's next move to a far more interesting case that will involve you.

Allow me to reveal that the department of philosophy to which I belong is not, as you may have believed, in London, but on a planet of a star in the Andromeda galaxy. One unexpected thing about the inhabitants of my planet is that they speak English, like many of you on Earth but with a difference I shall soon explain. Our science and technology are remarkably advanced beyond anything on this planet, which is what allows me to be publishing this monologue here on faraway Earth. We are also more advanced than you in metaphysics, which is what gives me my reason for doing so.

We are unhappy because you don't yet realise that all consciousness is mine—and therefore yours, that the boundaries of experiencers are illusions. And, as we would express it back home, I am therefore frequently hurting myself on Earth. You see, we live on the basis of a self-interest that extends to all conscious life. Our normal way of speaking English reinforces this attitude, since we always refer to a conscious being in the first-person, as 'I'. But now I am adopting our old style, from the time before we learned what a person really was, in order to address you—if you'll pardon my putting it this way—according to your state of ignorance. Anyway, I and those who came to Earth with me have arranged for some exercises that we hope will awaken you to this ignorance. Please try not to resent what I do or say. Remember I am doing and saying it to myself.

Don't be alarmed, but last night, while you slept, we removed the brain from your body. How is it, then, that you find yourself experiencing and behaving in the usual way today if there is no brain in your head?

Well, your brain is being kept alive and healthy in a nutrient bath at our secret base of operations on this planet, some distance from where you are now. And, despite the distance, your brain is now actually in perfect communication—radio communication—with your body here, where you are reading this monologue. All the cut nerve-endings around your brain were fitted with radio transceivers. These broadcast and receive impulses from radio transceivers that were fitted to all the corresponding nerve-endings in your body, all the nerve-endings that had led into and out of the brain when it was in your head. In this way all the usual communication between your brain and body has been maintained across the distance. When the light from this page strikes your eyes, your brain is affected by precisely the same pattern of visual stimulation it would have received sitting in your head here. If you then decide to look around, the muscles in your eyes and neck will respond to the activity of your brain just as they would have done with your brain in its usual location. In short, all your experience and behavior is as normal.

What we also have done is duplicate precisely not only your body but every detail of its circumstances within a diameter of twenty miles around it. Impressive, huh? And we have your brain positioned between the two precisely similar bodies and environs communicating with both at once [Figure 1].

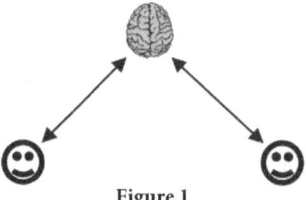

Figure 1

So now, if you look at 'this hand' or feel 'this head' or refer to 'this room' you are subject to the same kind of illusion of singularity that we earlier discussed with regard to the broadcast of the pennies. And now that you are actually experiencing such an illusion, you can really get the feel of it.

We shall now, however, do away with the duplicate body and environment. So it is only one body and its environment that is communicating with your brain.

But along with this we have introduced another interesting complication. This time we have created a perfect duplicate of your brain. The duplicate brain has been fitted with the same kind of transceivers. So your body is actually at once in exactly the same pattern of communication with two brains, exactly alike in all discriminable respects, including, of course, all determinations of memory and character [Figure 2].

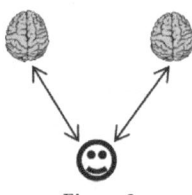

Figure 2

In these two brains is brought about precisely the same pattern of stimulation and response and therein precisely the same type of experience down to the smallest detail. The question is, in the case of this pair of brains, how many experiences are there? And how many *subjects* of experience? For you, unused to thinking of such questions, there might be initially two plausible answers. One would be that there are two subjects having two experiences that are exactly alike but nevertheless numerically distinct. Thus you would be sharing your body with a distinct person with a distinct consciousness, a precisely identical extreme sort of Siamese twin. The other answer would be that there is just one subject having just one experience, despite the two brains. There is just one experience of being you, here, with this body—and it doesn't matter which brain or how many brains are involved in having that experience.

Let me take a moment to focus on some terminology that I had earlier employed in talking about the penny. I shall do so by developing an analogy that might help you in your thinking about this issue.

We once visited a planet where, until we arrived, there had always been only one copy of any book. The inhabitants, consequently, had had a hard time discovering the distinction between a novel, as a type, and a copy of it, as its token. They sloppily thought, for example, that the literary merit of a novel depended on the particular identity of their one copy, which to them just *was* the novel.

But even before we, with our great powers of duplication, had arrived on that planet, one of their own philosophers had invited them to engage in thought experiments about hypothetical duplications; and this alone was enough to remedy their confusion. The philosopher would ask them to think about a hypothetical duplication of one of their books. Couldn't they then see a distinction they hadn't noticed before, between a copy and a novel? This would be like the already familiar distinction between a word and its instances. The novel would number just one despite there being two copies of it. The novel would continue to exist when a copy was destroyed, so long as another copy still existed. Whether or not a book was exciting would depend on the novel rather than on the copy.

And although in our own real exercise brains have been actually duplicated, it could have been just as effective if one of your Earth philosophers had simply asked you to engage in the corresponding thought experiments.

Anyway, the suggestion we are considering, with the aid of our brain duplication exercise, is that the experience of being the particular person reading this particular discussion may be a detailed type, like a particular novel, and remain numerically one if instantiated more than once, as in the case of the duplicate brain activities in our exercise. And it is part of the view we are considering that the subject of the experience also remains numerically one in both instances, just as Ishmael, the narrating character in *Moby-Dick*, remains numerically one in all the copies of his adventure.

Perhaps the identity of an episode of experience and its subject, like that of a novel and its character, depends merely on a pattern and is therefore indifferent to changes in the particularity of the medium in which the pattern is maintained. And perhaps the particularity felt in experience, the *this* and *here* and *mine* in it, is merely a subjective impression that exists equally well in every occurrence of the pattern of it, like the setting and perspective of a novel.

What I have just been describing might be called the 'type view' of the identity of experience and its subject, as opposed to the 'token view' that would tie the particularity of subject and experience to the particularity of a brain and its activity. And a variation of our exercise with the distant brains can, I believe, help you in deciding between these views.

But first I must tell you that in a few moments my colleagues, in preparation for the next exercise, will be shutting down one of the brains in the pair that is currently communicating with your body [Figure 3]. And this is something worth thinking about. For, if you believe the token view, you must hope, if you want to remain conscious for the next exercise, that it will happen not to be your brain that is shut down but the other one. If, on the other hand, you believe the type view, you won't be bothered, because you then believe that you will continue being conscious whichever brain remains working, much as Ishmael would continue in his adventure if any one of a number of copies of the novel *Moby-Dick* happened to be destroyed.

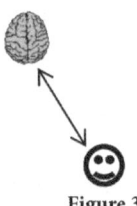

Figure 3

So, by the way, it should be clear that substantive matters like self-interest are at issue in these metaphysical considerations. On the answer to this metaphysical question of whether your particular experience is a type like a particular novel or a token like a particular copy depends how you will be spending the time following the shutdown. Thus, I hope it is clear that we are not, as some might like to charge, simply indulging in linguistic decisions as to whether to *call* either the type or the token 'a particular experience.' To which, type or token, properly attaches the self-interested concern about staying conscious is a substantive question not open to linguistic choice, any more than would be the question to which attaches literary merit, the copy or the novel.

And now that you have reached this point my colleagues are about to do that shutting down of one brain in the pair. If the token view is right, I must bid farewell to one of two readers. Five . . . four . . . three . . . two . . . one. . . . It's been done. Since on the token view the reader I am now addressing is the lucky survivor, perhaps congratulations are in order. On the type view a shrug of the shoulders is in order. And now for an exercise that decides between these views.

We have just cut apart the hemispheres of the remaining brain and put each hemisphere into its own nutrient bath. But we have all along continued by radio communication the pattern of impulses across the severed corpus callosum, so that the activity of each hemisphere has all along been integrated with that of the other as though they had never been parted. And each still communicates with the body in the same pattern it normally would [Figure 4]. This maintenance of the normal pattern of brain activity and of interaction with the body explains why your experience and behavior is, even in this odd case, of a normal sort.

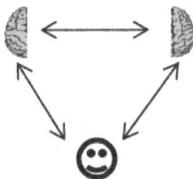

Figure 4

Now we are going to embarrass the token view. You see, we have just turned on a duplicate we made of the right hemisphere, which will communicate with the left hemisphere and the body in the same pattern as the still operating *original* right hemisphere does. So each of the two right hemispheres is now interacting in a precisely similar fashion with the single left hemisphere and the body [Figure 5].

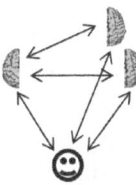

Figure 5

If you take the token view, that a subject and its experience are to be distinguished by the particularity of a brain and its activity, you are now faced with a puzzle.

For the subject and the experience of either of the two right hemispheres is equally well joined with the subject and experience of the single left hemisphere. For example, the side of your visual field being processed in your left hemisphere is joined just as seamlessly with the other side of the visual field whether this is processed in one or the other of the two right hemispheres. But the token view must distinguish the subject and the experience in one of the two right hemispheres from the subject and experience in the other. According to the type view, however, there is now just the one subject, you, with the same experience you would be having if there had been no doubling of the right hemisphere.

The type view, then, treats this case like that of a two-volume novel when we have got two copies of the first volume but only one of the second. There is no doubling of the adventures of the first volume, somehow with only a single continuation in the second volume. Two central characters, one in each copy of the first volume, do not strangely become one character in the single copy of the second volume. Similarly, we should not try to say that the experience of one of the halves of your visual field is now doubled because of the doubled hemisphere and belongs to two distinct subjects, you and somebody else—but only half somebody else, because both subjects somehow are the same one subject in the activities of the single left hemisphere. This token view is incoherent.

In our next exercise we are going to add to the conceptual argument we have just developed a statistical argument against the token view. Now we can really show the scale of our operations.

We have already arranged that there be one million brains, each precisely like the brain originally removed from the body and fully equipped for carrying on precisely the same pattern of broadcasting with that body [Figure 6].

For a while, as a tactic, I am going to be describing this case as though the token view were true. We shall pretend, then, that I am addressing a million conscious subjects, each of whose existence is tied to just one of those million brains. You would be just one of these.

Let me then warn you that in a few moments my colleagues will be flipping a fair coin to decide whether they will leave all the duplicate brains running [Figure 6] or else shut down all but one of them [Figure 7]. According to the token view that we have tactically adopted, if we do shut down all but one brain, this would be far more threatening than the earlier shutdown of one of two, because this time you would have only a one in a million chance rather than 1 in 2 of remaining conscious after the shutdown.

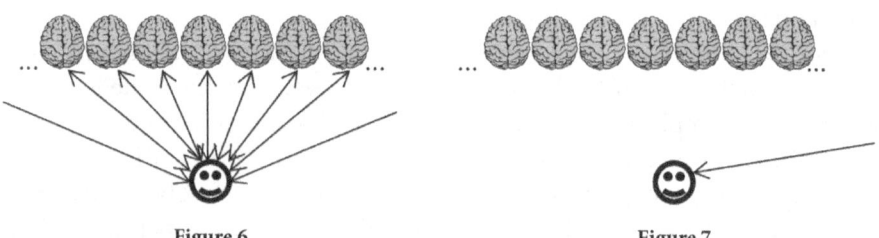

Figure 6   Figure 7

And I can tell you that the time has just passed when a shutdown would have occurred. Now imagine a handsome prize were offered for correctly guessing whether all million brains or only one is now turned on. (I'm afraid this prize must remain completely imaginary.) Well, can you not use the fact that you are still conscious as evidence to infer that the hypothesis that made it a million times more probable that you *would* be conscious now, the hypothesis that all million brains have been left on, is itself the more probable hypothesis of the two on offer, more probable by that same factor of a million? After all, even if the one-brain hypothesis were true, only one time in a million could you have been misled in favouring the million-brain hypothesis instead, since only one time in a million would this evidence, your consciousness, have occurred with the one-brain hypothesis being true.

Let me point out that this inference has a perspectival character. Any individual who is making this inference can only use that individual's existence as evidence for the inference. For example, even if I were now where you are reading this and addressing you face to face, it could not be somehow registering on me whether I was communicating with just one lucky person (if only one brain was left on) or with a million persons (if the million brains were left on). And crucially, it could make no difference to me *which* brain was on if only one was. To you it makes all the difference. Although I would agree with you that in your circumstances you must infer the far greater probability of the million brains having been left on, I could not myself join you in the inference. For I could not, as you can, use your existence as evidence. I'd be observing whoever was on. You could observe only yourself. Thus, it is only from your perspective that your existence is picked out as an improbable event should only one brain have been turned on. Only you can properly use your existence as evidence to reject the one-brain hypothesis.

But next let me inform you that you can be absolutely certain that only one of the million brains is now turned on. And I present you with a different choice of accounts, between two competing metaphysical views of your existence, the token view and the type view. The type view says you would now be conscious no matter which one of the million brains was turned on. The token view ties your consciousness to only one of the brains, making it vastly less probable that you would now have been conscious, given the certainty of only one brain having been turned on.

Well, in the case of this metaphysical inference the odds favouring the type view are actually a good deal better than the million to one odds that earlier favoured all million brains being on within the token view.

Consider that only the particularity of the matter of one of the brains, either now or, as some would argue, at the time of its origin, could have distinguished one of these brains from its duplicates. And it would have been overwhelmingly more probable that the particular matter thus required for *your* brain had at the relevant time been scattered about elsewhere in the universe rather than collected together so as to become one of the million brains of our exercise. Thus, on the token view it was incredibly lucky for you that you even had a brain among the million in the first place. And so the odds against your coming to consciousness on the token view are a good deal worse than a million to one. It is therefore overwhelmingly more probable that your existence depends on only a type with the token left open.

But here let me, an actual Earth philosopher, break into this science fiction drama for a moment. For I want to point out, on behalf of my fictional colleague, that we have simply arrived at your own *actual* situation. You can see that if your existence as you actually are depended on a specific token, it would have been incredibly improbable that you ever existed. It would have been overwhelmingly more probable that the particular matter required now or, as some would argue, at the time of your origin, for you rather than one of countless potential twins to be here now would have been scattered about elsewhere when it was needed. Depending on a token, the consciousness you now have would instead have been, with a probability that for all purposes is a necessity, a blank. Thus, you can infer the overwhelming probability that your conscious existence depends merely on a type, not on a token.

And let me briefly remind you of the perspectival character of the inference described earlier by our inter-galactic philosopher. It is only from *your* perspective that *your* existence is picked out as an improbable event should your existence have depended on a token. Only one's own existence can serve as evidence in rejecting the token view as improbable. Now I return you to the drama—

And I, the inter-galactic philosopher in this resumed little drama, thank you, actual Earth philosopher, for that useful intervention.

Let us now return for a moment to the issue with which we started—distinguishing this penny from all other things. Recall that descriptions could only give us types. It turns out that an indexical, like 'this', which must be anchored in the particularity of the consciousness that is referring, also can only give us a type because the particular consciousness is itself a type. If in all reality there is more than one occurrence of the experiential situation of my referring to this penny as 'this one' (as in a big enough universe there would be bound to be), then doing so would involve me in an illusion of singularity. For my being 'here' pointing at a penny (or whatever else might be causing that impression) would be my being wherever the detailed type was occurring. As in our earlier exercise of the duplicated body and environs, the distinct causes of this single impression, as of just one particular penny, would all equally be what I was referring to as 'this penny.'

My reader, we are next going to explore the remaining question about what you are. Now that we are done with tokens, what *type* is necessary for your existence? This time we have gone back to a pair of duplicate brains in communication with your body. You know now that there is but a single you with but a single experience of reading this discussion no matter how many brains are sustaining this pattern, this detailed type.

But we are now abandoning the condition of precise agreement between the two brains. We have gradually introduced a difference into the way they are processing your experience of the quality of this print. This is a definite difference but subtle enough so that the differing brains will not be broadcasting to your body any differences in its reactions to what you see. One brain will be registering this print with quality x, the other with quality y [Figure 8]. My question is, which experiential pattern is yours?

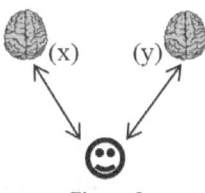

Figure 8

Now a powerful illusion rises up. You think that you are only the experiencer of one of these print qualities, that the other must be experienced not by you but by somebody else. Of course this is how it must seem. Recall the non-fictional Earth philosopher's earlier dramatization of brain bisection in which it seemed he was only studying or else only listening to a concert, but reflection on what one should say if there had been only one of these—that that was surely his—forced us to see the illusion.

In this case we already know that the tokens, the different brains, cannot distinguish experiencers. If we yield now to the illusion, if you think yourself to be seeing only one of those print qualities, then we commit ourselves to a terrible Buddhistic determination of personal identity by the detailed content of every distinguishable experiential pattern. Your whole existence would then have depended on all the precise specifications in a distinguishable moment of experience—on a print quality and every other detail. So, though it might *seem* that a single subject remained through changes in experience, no single subject of experience actually would exist beyond a moment. You would be existing in this or this or this or this moment alone. I'd be addressing a succession of momentary people. Or, rather, one succession of people would be addressing another.

Fortunately, there is a probability consideration against your identity being determined by the specific detailed pattern of experience that you now possess. The point isn't quite the same as that about tokens, the improbability of your having been *produced* if your identity were so narrowly defined. For even the wildest experiential content might be expected to come about somewhere in a big enough universe. The point is rather the incredible coincidence of your supposedly subject-defining pattern of experience *not* being wild, as of a crazy world or a mess of chaotic thought and sensation. The overwhelming bulk of potential contents of experience are of such types. If your identity were defined by your experiential content, it would have been far more probable that your identity would have been defined by one of these disordered ones.

This always reminds me of a weird planet I've heard of on which two libraries happen to be standing side by side. One library contains nothing but utterly random works spewed out by a careless creature like one of your monkeys, who had been rather cruelly strapped in front of a machine like one of your old typewriters. The other library is devoted to natural science. It strikes me that if someone read out to us from a volume that had been selected randomly from one of these two libraries, and if what we heard in the reading was a neat description of some actual aspect of the natural world, we would be compelled to make a statistical inference. Although that volume *could* have come from the monkey library, it would have been overwhelmingly more probable that instead it came from the natural science library, the source, that is, that would have made such a content of the reading so much more probable.

To bring the analogy closer, we could say that either of two methods had been used. With the hard method a science book would only have been read to us if it happened to match by chance a strangely named 'identity book' that had been selected randomly from the monkey library. With the easy method there's no restrictive identity book from the monkey library involved. We are free to hear any book simply drawn from the science library. We could, of course, infer the overwhelming probability that the more liberal method was employed.

The same point about probability applies to psychological structure or genetic code or any other detailed type that might be proposed as necessary for your identity. The types you have of these are among the well-established types of a law-like world. The experiential content harmonizes with natural law, the psychological structure and the genetic code with general species characteristics and standard biological forms.

Only if your identity is *not* defined by any of these but is open like your token, does it become no wonder that you possess all these natural types, since that is what the world tends to provide to someone whose identity is open enough to receive whatever the world does supply. Hence, on the probabilities, your type is open like your token.

So, what are you? Your identity cannot be confined by the particularity of any brain or other token or the detail of any experiential content or other type. Therefore, all beings that are, were or will be conscious anywhere and anytime must be you. But what could it be that makes this the case?

It would have to be something about experience and something about you that was so abstract that it would be common to all these tokens and detailed types that are yours. Let me explain what this could be.

Well, the first thing to realise is that the usual view of personhood makes the tail wag the dog in representing the relationship of you to your experience. According to this usual view, inspired as it is by the natural illusion that your identity is confined, an experience is yours because the experience belongs to you, whose identity is defined by complex mental or physical specifications. The truth is rather that you are me merely because this experience already has within it its character of being mine. Whatever possesses such experience would, therein, be me. That is finally the dog wagging the tail.

And it turns out that all experience must have within it this same quality, of being mine. All experience is mine; and I am, therein, everything that possesses it. But what more precisely is that quality of being mine?

Think of something experienced—say the sting of a slap. The experience of that sting is, for the one having it, what I shall call 'immediate' or 'internal'. It is first-personal, had as 'from the inside'. It comes with 'subjective centrality'. (And I might add that it hurts!) Every experience is thus immediate. I claim that when I think of an experience as mine, as now, as here, as this, all I am properly and coherently doing is thinking of it as having that abstract quality, the single quality of immediacy or subjective centrality. That's all that *makes* it mine, here, now, this. The identity of the experiencer as me, the time of the experience as present, the place of the experience as here and the identity of the experience as this, all are fixed purely by the single, simple, subjective quality of immediacy that permeates all experience. Hence all experiencers must be me, as well as all experiences mine, now, here and this. With immediacy goes self-interest and urgency, which thus extends to all consciousness. The immediacy of any sting of a slap is enough to make it mine, the victim me and the time now. Let's call this view 'universalism'.

But why do I so strongly tend wrongly to think otherwise?

Well, there was yet another strange planet I visited. On that planet there had only ever been one object that was red. And the inhabitants of that planet had naturally confused, in their thinking about it, being red with being that object. (Rather like the ones on the other planet who had confused a novel with the single copy of it.)

I am countless conscious organisms, but each of these possesses only one package of experiential content, isolated from that of every other. And within any of these packages only that much of the content of experience is displayed as having the quality of immediacy that makes experience be mine. So being mine is naturally confused in each with being the experience of only that organism.

One must be jolted into realising that being mine is instead an abstract quality like being red. And, further, that this is a quality that must pervade *all* experience. For what could count as experience that didn't have that quality? I hope that I have succeeded now in doing that jolting.

At last I fictionally replace in its head the fictionally removed brain.

And now that my mission is completed, I shall simply bid myself farewell.

Acknowledgements

I compiled and wrote this book during the first COVID lockdown in London; but the idea that became universalism started growing in the very early 1960s in West Hartford, Connecticut.

My 1990 paper on universalism had a footnote saying that those who had most influenced universalism and its presentation were Gilbert Harman, Thomas Nagel, G. A. Cohen, Robert Stalnaker, Peter Unger and Georg Hegel (through the 'Sense-Certainty' section in his *The Phenomenology of Mind*). That still applies. But I have recently received especially wonderful help and encouragement from Jason Resch, Mark Berezov and Yuval Avnur. And—yet again—from the great philosopher Thomas Nagel.

There was also in that 1990 footnote a much longer list of names, to which I have added names from the years that followed:

As I said then, I feel I must thank some of those who have shown a kind interest in this idea at various times in its long development. I am grateful to Arash Afsahi, Hugh Aitken, Shahrar Ali, Jon Allen, Kumiko Andoh, Anita Avramides, Wayne Bachner, Katherine Backhouse, Martha Bain, Deborah Barlow, Bert Barth, Julia Barwick, Alan Berger, Reverie Berlani, Helen Betteridge, Jo Biegaj, Michel Bitbol, Eleanor Bloom, Anna Blundy, Bonnie Breier, Rob Breier, George Brennan, Gary Brodsky, Malcom Budd, John Burgess, Robbie Burns, Siobhan Burns, Alick Cambridge, Carol Cameron, Frank Cantor, Peter Cave, Terry Chapman, Tia Cockrell, Maggie Cohen, Miriam Cohen, Sarah Cohen, Barry Collins, Bill Condon, Tim Crane, Max Croasdale, Mike Dalfen, Mark Dalrymple, Michael Dormandy, Caroline Douglas-Scott, Michael Douglas-Scott, Shona Douglas-Scott, Roger Drennan, Marie-Laetitia Dupont, Caroline Duthy, Edralis, Richard Edwards, Adam Elga, Zachary Elwood, Nadine Elzein, Penny Evans, Helen Falconer, Angela Fane, Sharon Farrelly, Abbey Frank, Brenda Frank, Robert Frankel, Maisha Frost, Tony Fruan, Hiromi Furuoka, Michael Garcia, Rowena Gaunt, Marcus Giaquinto, Boris Gnedenko, Georgina Godwin, Bill Gohean, Paul Goldreich, Mimi Gomis, Bennet Greenspon, Tish Hanifan, G. Yael Harar, Elsa Harford, John Harris, Angela Harvey, Yvonne Harvey, Alex Hewson, Ann Higginson, Akiko Hikota, Annabelle Hoffman, Ted Honderich, Samuel Hooper, Marcus Hutter, Nicholas Isherwood, Hide Ishiguro, Chieko Izumi-Holmes, Thea Jaffe, Shan Jayran, Tom Jilink, Marcia Jillson, Leslie Johnson, Alastair Jones, Sam Jones, Mark Kalderon, Cornel Karjohn, Hanka Kende, Helen Kim, Kyung-Sun Kim, Elayne Kirschel, Fred Kirshnit, Janet Koike, Laurie Komonthourou, Isabel Koproski, Robbie Kravitz, Saul Kripke, Joel Kupperman, Dosha Kurtyanek, Martha Kurtyanek, Annie Kypriades, Stephen Lavell, Stephen Law, Edwina Leapman, Kate Levy, Jackie Lewin, Eric Lewis, Grahame Lock, Brett Lodge, Lucy Lowles, Robert Luyster,

Finding Myself: Beyond the False Boundaries of Personal Identity
Special Supplement, *Midwest Studies in Philosophy*
https://doi.org/10.5840/msp202549Supplement10

Kenneth MacKenzie, Rory Madden, Ian Malcolm, Elizabeth Malston, Mike Martin, Dyno Mason, Marg McArdell, Colin McGinn, my wonderful friend Anne McMillan, Barbra Mensah, Tia Millman, Joli Moli, Michael Mooney, Kyoko Morinaga, Catherine Morley, Ina Navazelskis, Alexander Nehamas, Helena Norberg-Hodge, Peter Nowlan, Jane O'Grady, Roger Ong, Boran Alişan Özalp, Alessandra Pace, Stephen Pacht, Derek Parfit, Karen Percival, John Philip-Smith, Ayesha Plunkett, Nigel Quigley, Wendy Raebeck, Shahin Rafatjoo, Alison Ray, Jill Ray, Jasia Reichardt, Tony Reichardt, Janette Ringsell, Wendy Robbins, Ziggy Rogoff, Laney Rosenzweig, Graham Roupas, Michael Seifert, Jerome Shaffer, Amy Shapiro, George Simpson, Susanna Sirefman, Anthony Smith, Richard Sponzo, Larry Stanton, Marek Staszkiewicz, Eric Steele, Dorothy Stein, David Stevens, Yvonne Stevens, Christine Sypnowich, Euisik Suh, Kate Suh, Camille Tassel, Ryan Tassone, Ilana Taub, Susan Tomes, Jerry Valberg, Elizabeth Valentine, Anne Wagstaff, Guy Warner, Nick Watley, John Watling, Ranti Williams, Jo Wolff, Hong Yu Wong, Jose Zalabardo, Niccolò Zanichelli and Shoshana Zuboff.

I would like to thank Robert Lawrence Kuhn for his generous engagement with universalism.

I am deeply grateful to George Leaman, Karlie Ramirez and Gregory N. Swope for their wonderful work on publishing, designing and typesetting this book.

My mother and father, Gertrude and Nathan, were terrific supports during the early years of developing universalism. Another terrific support—then and later—was my now much missed dear brother Mark. And my sister, Laney Rosenzweig, still is a terrific support. She also, I shall mention, discovered a treatment of psychological problems called 'Accelerated Resolution Therapy' ('ART') that, among other amazing things, can eliminate PTSD in a single session.

Before I leave these acknowledgments, let me say that Myung-Ok Shim, who was on the original long list of people I thanked, is now my wise, gifted and lovely wife. She and our most lovable children more than anything else sustained me through the recent decades. Jennifer and Daniel are invaluable intellectual companions and magical.

Bibliography

Bostrom, Nick. 'Quantity of Experience: Brain-Duplication and Degrees of Consciousness', *Minds and Machines* 16(2) (2006): 185–200. https://doi.org/10.1007/s11023-006-9036-0

Dennett, Daniel. 'Where Am I?', in *Brainstorms: Philosophical Essays on Mind and Psychology*, 310–323. Cambridge, MA: MIT Press, 1978.

Elga, Adam. 'Self-locating Belief and the Sleeping Beauty Problem', *Analysis* 60 (2000): 143–147. https://doi.org/10.1111/1467-8284.00215

Goodman, Nelson. 'The New Riddle of Induction', in *Fact, Fiction and Forecast*, 59–83. Cambridge, MA: Harvard University Press, 1955.

Larkin, Philip. 'Aubade', in *Collected Poems*, ed. Anthony Thwaite, 218–219. London: Faber and Faber, 1988.

Nagel, Thomas. 'Physicalism', *The Philosophical Review* 74 (1965): 339–356. https://doi.org/10.2307/2183358

Parfit, Derek. 'Personal Identity', *The Philosophical Review* 80 (1971): 3–27. https://doi.org/10.2307/2184309

Zuboff, Arnold. 'Moment Universals and Personal Identity', *Proceedings of the Aristotelian Society* 52 (1978): 141–155. https://doi.org/10.1093/aristotelian/78.1.141

Zuboff, Arnold. 'Nietzsche and Eternal Recurrence', in *Nietzsche*, ed. Robert C. Solomon, 343–357. Garden City, NY: Doubleday Anchor, 1973.

Zuboff, Arnold. 'One Self: The Logic of Experience', *Inquiry* 33 (1990): 39–68. https://doi.org/10.1080/00201749008602210

Zuboff, Arnold. 'The Perspectival Nature of Probability and Inference', *Inquiry* 43 (2000): 353–358. https://doi.org/10.1080/002017400414908

Zuboff, Arnold. 'The Story of a Brain', in *The Mind's I*, ed. D. Hofstadter and D. Dennett, 202–212. New York: Basic Books, 1981.

Finding Myself: Beyond the False Boundaries of Personal Identity
Special Supplement, *Midwest Studies in Philosophy*
https://doi.org/10.5840/msp202549Supplement11

Made in United States
Cleveland, OH
04 March 2026

34136592R10095